A SCHOOL ANSWERS BACK:
Responding to Student Drug Use

by
Richard A. Hawley

the American Council for Drug Education

5820 Hubbard Drive
Rockville, Maryland 20852
301.984.5700

136 East 64th Street
New York, New York 10021
212.758.8060

The American Council for Drug Education is a non-profit membership organization dedicated to public education about the health hazards of various psychoactive substances. CDE promotes research, organizes conferences, reviews scientific findings, and educates the public about current knowledge of the effects of drug use.

Since its founding in 1977, CDE has been dedicated to the principle that an informed public is the nation's best defense against drug abuse. While knowledge alone will not solve the drug problem, there is now abundant evidence that it will help to reduce drug experimentation and even drug use among people of all ages – including teenagers. Furthermore, public understanding of the health consequences of drug use is the necessary precondition to a wide range of family, community, religious, cultural, legal and other efforts to deal with drug abuse problems. In the absence of clear, reliable and objective information about the health effects of drugs, the prevention of drug abuse in our society is all but impossible.

Copyright © 1984 The American Council for Drug Education
Library of Congress Catalog Card Number: 83-073198
ISBN: 942348-14-1

CONTENTS

ABOUT THE AUTHOR iv
ACKNOWLEDGMENTS v
PREFACE vi
A NOTE TO THE READER vii

PART ONE: THE CONCEPT

ACKNOWLEDGING A DRUG PROBLEM 1
STEMMING AN EPIDEMIC OF
    STUDENT DRUG USE: STARTING 8
GETTING STARTED IN SCHOOL:
    FACULTY FIRST 13
TRAINING STAFF TO RECOGNIZE
    AND RESPOND TO STUDENT DRUG USE 15
ESTABLISHING A SCHOOL-FAMILY PARTNERSHIP
    IN TREATING DRUG CONCERNS 24
REFERRAL TO TREATMENT 27
REINCORPORATING RECOVERING USERS 32
RULES AND DISCIPLINE: SHAPING THE
    CLIMATE OF CONSEQUENCES IN WHICH
    STUDENTS DECIDE ON DRUG USE 35
PREVENTING STUDENT DRUG USE:
    EDUCATION AND INFORMATION 43
STARTING A PARENT AWARENESS NETWORK 52

PART TWO: A STORY

THE ADVENT OF DRUG USE: THE SETTING 73
EXPERIENCING STUDENT DRUG USE:
    THE EXPERIMENT TAKES HOLD 84
UNDERSTANDING STUDENT DRUG USE 100
RESPONDING TO STUDENT DRUG USE:
    ANSWERING BACK 110
BRIGHT SIGNS 141

ABOUT THE AUTHOR

Dr. Richard A. Hawley is Director of the University School, Hunting Valley Campus, Chagrin Falls, Ohio. A 1967 graduate of Middlebury College, he was awarded a doctorate in political science by Case Western Reserve University. Dr. Hawley also received a masters in theology from St. John's College, Cambridge University.

Richard Hawley is a distinguished author, poet, and educator whose work has been published in numerous reviews, quarterlies, and papers, as well as in two anthologies, *The Yearbook Of American Magazine Verse* and *Light Year*. His articles on the role of the teacher, the effects of television on the adolescent, and the impact of marijuana on the school have appeared in such magazines as *The Atlantic Monthly, Phi Delta Kappan, Education Digest,* and *American Film.* Dr. Hawley is the author of several books and monographs, including *The Purposes of Pleasure: A Reflection on Youth and Drugs.*

ACKNOWLEDGMENTS

Without a wide variety of help, even as modest a volume as this one could not have been written. The research, editorial assistance, and informed technical judgments of my colleague Margaret Mason, school psychologist at University School, have been invaluable. I am also grateful to a number of administrators and counselors from schools across the country for supplying especially helpful information: Robert Miller, Thacher School (California); Janet Davis, Cate School, (California); Al Deimidio, E. P. DuPont High School (Delaware); Terry Barton, New Trier High School East (Illinois); Katharine Saltonstall, Tabor Academy (Massachusetts).

From greater Cleveland, we had generous help from many sources, including Nancy Taylor, Cleveland Heights High School; Richard Peterjohn, Shaker Heights High School; Rabbi Moerman, Hebrew Academy; Mr. Michael Bova, Baptist Christian School; Sister Margaret Mary Lyons, Villa Angela School; and Sister Martha, O.S.U., Beaumont School. Also of special interest locally were various drug awareness materials produced by The Community Intervention workshops in Cleveland, as was a study of student drug use produced for the Catholic Diocese of Cleveland by Robert Mlaker and Robert Stec.

To Eileen Standfield, skilled decipherer, speedy typist, and superb organizer, go special thanks.

Inevitably, I have had to recount some actual, specific events my colleagues and I experienced at school over the past fifteen years. In every instance, the names of the people involved, and in a few cases some of the circumstances, have been changed to protect the anonymity of their referents.

Finally—and once again—I am indebted to the students, parents, and faculty of University School for providing the kind of learning climate in which any question may be asked, any problem tackled. In such a community there is always hope for brighter things ahead.

R.A.H.
Chagrin Falls, 1983

PREFACE

Richard Hawley, Director of the Upper School at University School, outside of Cleveland, Ohio has written a book which is important for anyone concerned about youth in America today. In it, Dr. Hawley describes his own school's difficult but productive efforts to confront drug and alcohol abuse. He reaches beyond his own experience to draw on the rapidly growing body of knowledge about drug abuse prevention to offer guidelines for school communities, both public and private. Here is a literate, accurate and inspirational book, written by a talented teacher and published poet, to help us cope with the drug abuse epidemic.

My own background in medicine and health promotion for youth ranging from many years as a professor of pediatrics and child psychiatry to developing the Head Start Program and four years as the U.S. Surgeon General, has taught me that drug and alcohol abuse pose a major threat to our children's health, well-being, and capacity to learn. A 1983 Gallup poll of American teenagers showed that youth go even farther: they ranked drug abuse as the Number One threat to their generation. In fact, they saw it as twice as serious as unemployment, the second highest ranked problem.

I also have learned that the most complex problems often respond to surprisingly straightforward solutions. Hawley demonstrates that this is certainly true for drug abuse. He shows us that prevention begins with a clear understanding of the nature, causes, and cures of the problem and that the greatest danger is *denial*— the tendency to think "drugs are someone else's problem." The "answer" Hawley develops is based on a sense of positive community involvement, with active roles defined for everyone in the school as well as for the student's family.

During the course of this approach, we should learn much more about how habituation may be prevented.

It is within the context of this positive, health-promoting community where everyone works together to establish a central, shared goal: helping youth grow up free of drug dependence. Hawley's book is an important milestone in our nation's effort to achieve that goal.

> Dr. Julius Richmond
> Director, Division of Health
>   Policy Research and Education
> Harvard University

A NOTE TO THE READER:

Basic Assumptions

This book is written for school staff, parents, and others interested in confronting and reversing the use of drugs by developing children. Whoever may initiate the response to student drug use, the school must ultimately become an active partner in the effort. If a school should take the lead in the drug education of a community, so much the better. Since a school's job, intelligent voices have argued, is to pass on the arts and sciences of the culture and to promote good citizenship, isn't drug abuse prevention just another social failing left at the school's doorstep? Decidedly not. As Neil Postman and others have pointed out in their recent educational writing, prior to the process of teaching anything is the creation of an atmosphere in which the process can take place. The past decade's epidemic—and "epidemic" is the technically correct word—of youthful drug use has impaired the learning of millions of children, including many who have not themselves used illicit drugs. While not a problem of their own making, the "drug problem" must be addressed and resolved by schools or they will continue to be frustrated in their primary mission.

This book has been divided into two halves, called "The Concept" and "A Story." The first is intended to serve as a blueprint for schools that wish to start a drug program or that wish to augment what has already been started. The provisions and suggestions in this section have been taken both from my colleagues' and my experiences at University School, Cleveland, and from the experiences of other public and independent schools across the country. Without, I hope, being too rigid and prescriptive, the first section provides a stage-by-stage program by which a school might structure itself to become drug free.

The second section, "A Story," recounts how in the course of my own experience at University School, we came to acknowledge a "drug problem," then to respond to it. Although there have been some gratifying results of our particular struggle against student drug use, we have proceeded in what has at times been a quixotic and ineffectual manner; in other words, we have made mistakes. It is hoped that by showing actual experiences, even unhappy and wrong-headed ones, other schools can see not only the desirability but the possibility of reversing the current involvement with drugs on the part of the young. In other words, our "story" does not show a best or even superior way to counter drug use, but it does show a way.

Underlying both sections of the book are some important assumptions that are best made explicit from the outset. These might at first glance seem severe or "unrealistic," but on reflection will be seen to be essential to effective drug abuse prevention. The first assumption is that there are no important distinctions among the various drugs as to which is more dangerous. Children can and do become destructively dependent on any drug which alters experience pleasurably. Every drug treatment facility in the country is aware of this, but teachers, parents, and students typically are not. It is possible to become as chronically dependent on pot as on heroin. Alcohol (a nervous system depressant) is not by any measure a less serious danger to the health and maturation of children than other mood-altering chemicals. Alcohol use is a substantial component of the current "drug problem"; in no way does alcohol use by developing children constitute a separate or lesser problem.

Another assumption is that the prevention of student drug use will succeed only if the school, with the support of the community, is aiming to become drug free. Drawing distinctions between the "use" and "abuse" of illicit drugs serves only to support illicit drug use which in consequence leads to a predictable measure of abuse. That such claims are even made—e.g., that there are "responsible" levels of drug use for children and "responsible use" ought to be the social goal, not repressive "prohibition"—are here regarded as signs of how far the impact of the youthful drug culture has progressed. "Responsible use" is a notion worth examining. The most recent national survey data suggest that the age of "first time" use of illicit substances is most likely to occur between ages twelve and sixteen, in spite of the fact that alcohol and all other substances most commonly used are expressly forbidden for that age group by law. With respect to both cultural tradition and written statutes, alcohol and other drug use by children is as illicit as underage driving, as stealing from a store, or as vandalism. And while social forces have not yet, so far as I know, coalesced to urge "moderate" amounts of underage driving, theft, and mayhem, such forces have been mobilized to advocate moderate amounts of a demonstrably more destructive practice: taking illicit chemicals—all of them toxic—for pleasure. To state it plainly, since drug use bears destructively on important processes in developing children, the advocates of children must oppose drug use unequivocally. To do less is not to respect the "rights" or "liberties" of children (no one in the Western World, child or not, has the "right" to break laws in the pursuit of chemical pleasure, and, as addicts at least know, nothing curtails liberty more surely than drug taking); to do less is only to respect the place drugs have made for themselves in contemporary society.

In the pages that follow, readers will be invited to consider the "record" of youthful drug involvement, especially marijuana and alcohol, over the past two decades. From no standpoint, except possibly from the economic standpoint of drug sellers, is the record something one can be proud of. From an educational or public health standpoint, it is an appalling record. Setting it right is not only desirable, it is culturally imperative. What follows is intended to demonstrate that it is also possible.

Richard A. Hawley

PART ONE:
THE CONCEPT

1.

ACKNOWLEDGING A DRUG PROBLEM

"Is there a drug problem in your school?"
The question is no longer a novelty for school teachers and administrators. School boards, concerned parents, newspaper and television reports all have come to ask the question of American middle schools and high schools. There is no region of the country in which the question is not asked. The question is asked in both the richest and poorest communities in the United States. It is asked routinely of public, private, and parochial schools. It was never asked before nineteen sixty-five; today everyone asks.

The question is typically answered in several ways. Perhaps the most common is: "Well, I suppose there is some drug use here by a minority of students, and there is some drinking, but there is not really a problem." While agreeable-sounding in certain respects (some drug use is acknowledged, but no worrying consequences), this answer is almost never true. National survey data[1] and school's own surveys say otherwise. Another answer, one given recently by the headmaster of a distinguished New England boarding school to *Wall Street Journal* reporters who had pointed to extensive drug dealing among its students was, "I know of no drug use in the school." This statement is undoubtedly true; the headmaster indeed does not know of any drug use in his school. Another answer—"Yes, there is widespread drug use in our school, we detect very little of it, yet it is undermining student competence, faculty morale, and the community's support for education"—is rarely given, although it is often true.

[1] Johnson, Bachman, and O'Malley, Drugs and the Nation's High School Students, National Institute of Drug Abuse (1982).

Why the ignorance? Why the denial? The reason for the misleading and unsatisfactory responses to "drug"-related inquiries lies in the very nature of drug taking. Practically all intoxicating substances are illegal to school-aged youth, and many of them are illegal, or else strictly controlled, for the adult population as well. Student use and exchange of drugs is therefore necessarily a furtive business. Furtiveness is what parents and teachers see first, not joints raised to lips, pills popped, or slugs taken from cans and bottles. Moreover, not all drugs impair motor coordination dramatically; many cannot be smelled or otherwise sensed. Parents and teachers often miss early signs of drug use or attribute it to "normal" teenage experimentation or to typical adolescent behavior. Finally, and perhaps the greatest obstacle to recognizing student drug problems, is the fact that it is no fun to do it. Confronting a stoned-looking child about drug use elicits fear (from the confronter as well as the confronted), anger, and a full range of repercussions ranging from heated, often defensive meetings with parents, the confrontive person's being labeled a 'narc' or an otherwise enemy to youth, even to serious legal action. These are not inconsiderable factors. Their like has driven fine teachers out of teaching. It is far easier to let the drowsy kid dream on in the back of the room or to chalk up the student's pungent breath at the school dance to a curious mouthwash. Even successful drug confrontations involve anxious risk taking, strong feelings, bad feelings, and many hours of time. Confronting drug problems is done as poorly and as infrequently as it is because it is very demanding. There is no certainty that the effort, even if undertaken, will pay off. Perhaps the only reliable motive for acknowledging, and then taking on, the "drug problem" is a love of actual children and a commitment to their development.

Acknowledging a problem is the first step. Data—in student performance, attitude, appearance—cannot be ignored. Nationally, the data suggest an epidemic problem. The data across the teacher's desk or across the dinner table often confirm the suggestion. Over the past five years, between one in ten and one in fourteen high school seniors has indicated using marijuana (an increasingly potent hallucinogen) every day. A majority of high school students report using marijuana less frequently. A great majority of students report periodic alcohol intoxication (not just "use"), and significant numbers of school-aged youth report some use of other drugs, most commonly LSD, PCP, cocaine, methaqualone (Quaalude®),

Acknowledging A Drug Problem

amphetamine, and inhalable solvents. In sum, middle schoolers and older students have evolved into a social pattern in which drinking is standard, drug experimentation likely, and drug dependence common. In the two-decade period over which this pattern has emerged, student aptitude and competence has declined substantially, as measured by the nationally administered Scholastic Aptitude Test (S.A.T.). Within months of the time of writing (1983), two extensive studies of the Nation's secondary schools have pronounced them in a state of crisis and disarray.

The decline in student competence and in the educational quality of schools happens to coincide perfectly with the incidence of psychoactive drug use in this country. This is no mystery. Intoxicating chemicals work: they produce altered feeling states. They act on the cells and tissue, including the brain. Cells and tissues are altered, damaged—sometimes irreversibly—by these substances. Because the changes and damage are often accompanied by intense pleasure, users are willing to risk losses, some even to the point of addiction and death. This is the "drug problem." Sensual pleasures, which have evolved over millenia to foster survival, procreation, and achievement, can now be called upon, irresistibly and toxically, through the use of pleasure-producing substances. In other words drugs can make the powerful primary reward system of the brain "pay off" without a biologically or socially necessary achievement.

Drugs are usually classed as depressants, which slow or block neurological activity (i.e., alcohol, opiates); as stimulants, which facilitate or speed up neurological activity (i.e., amphetamine, cocaine); or as hallucinogens, which alter the ways in which sensory information is processed (i.e., LSD, peyote, cannabis derivatives). Drugs are taken for a kick—to feel good or at least better. The biochemical action of the drug, including damage, may not be experienced consciously at all. Think of it: drugs block or change the intake of information, they scramble the processing of information, and they interfere with responses to information (through slowed response, incomplete understanding, loss of coordination, etc.). And again, many drugs act on the very centers which would inform one about a drug-related loss. Thus a drug abuser, and only a drug abuser, is unlikely to acknowledge and attach feelings to failing, losing family and friends, committing crimes for the first time, being chronically ill, or even starving. All of the processes with which drugs interfere are crucial to learning and to maturation. School-aged children going through intensive periods of learning and maturation are therefore most susceptible to drug-related losses. From the onset of their pubescence children are challenged to master and channel intense feelings. If in this process they take drugs which both break down controls over feelings and infuse users with irresistibly pleasurable feelings, maturation will be stunted. Children in developed cultures are exposed through education to a program of increasingly complex operations. Drugs in all classifications break down complexity—as well as the ability to sequence steps, to attend, and to form hypotheses. Drugs and education are therefore antithetical. School-aged children using drugs, including alcohol, constitute a "drug problem."

In many ways this news—that drugs are bad for learning and maturation—is obvious. Yet it can be too disturbing; the very magnitude of the problem can lead one to deny the problem or to bark up a more familiar tree. Over the past decade there has been barking up every conceivable wrong tree. Here is the "liberal-with-it"[2] tree: *Drug use is a symptom, not the cause of the child's/school's problems. Get that kid rapping meaningfully with his father (mother, brother, sister, friends, coach) again and he/she won't need drugs. Moreover, get that school to provide relevant, engaging classroom activity and you'll find those kids more involved in science and literature and less involved in drugs.* Sometimes even: *With a society as routinized/mechanized/commercialized/repressive as this one, little wonder kids try drugs instead. Provide a healthful world in which youth have meaningful challenges and genuine relationships, and you won't have to worry about a "drug problem."* Perhaps you have heard some of this. At its nub it says drug use by children is not a primary problem; the primary problem is _____, for which young people resort to drug use. Resolve the primary problem, and poof!, goodbye drugs. This is sensible sounding, but wrong. The fact of the matter is that the various ills named as primary problems—an unfeeling parent, a dull curriculum, a painful divorce, a commercial/repressive, etc. society—were all culturally manifest prior to the epidemic in psychoactive drug use by youth. For decades in this century school life progressed with larger class sizes, more uniform curriculum, behavioral regimentation, yet there was no massive public outcry. Nor, over those decades were there staff psychologists in schools,

[2]This kind of "liberalism" bears no relationship to any development of political thought.

a well-developed structure of child psychiatry, a burgeoning industry in chemical dependency treatment centers. This is not to deny primary problems. Primary problems—divorces, rejections, etc.—are real enough, but they are, in healthy development, an occasion for adaptation, growth, or workable defenses. Anesthetize the primary problem with a drug, and none of those responses will occur. On this point the Alcoholics Anonymous organization has always been clear: whatever the underlying psychological problem marked by alcohol, one will not get at it until the alcoholism is addressed. Until that happens, alcoholism *is* the primary problem. Similarly, until the student drug problem is addressed and corrected, we will not know what the "primary" problems of contemporary school life are. Until then, drug use is the primary problem.

There are other wrong trees. Prominent among them is the "conservative/out-of-it"[3] tree. This point of view might be summarized in the following way: *Of course there is a drug problem among kids. It's the natural outgrowth of too much permissiveness. The permissiveness started after World War II when that whole baby boom generation was raised on Dr. Spock who said children are entitled to what they want when they want it. That's the generation that opened the door to drugs, and that's the generation raising the kids who are in school today. They grew up expecting Instant Gratification—and now they've got it in the form of the "drug problem."* This rather irritable view seems to contain a germ of plausibility. Like the "liberal/with-it" doctrine, it fixes blame on a benighted other party: a massive, hazily defined social force (the "repressive" or the "permissive") who are responsible for the problem. Accordingly, the problem won't go away until they go away or change. And, like its "liberal" counterpart, the "conservative" view is also shot through with faulty information and poor logic. Dr. Spock never advocated giving infants what they wanted when they wanted it. Nor did the post-war generation become immediately druggy upon passing into adolescence. In fact, this very generation emerged into a kind of "golden age" of adolescence, a decade between the middle 1950s and the middle 1960s, which might be characterized as "the Fifties": an overall placid, orderly span of years in which, in the stereotyped images of press and emergent television, the U.S.A. was the undisputed leader of the Free World, elementary students across the country began the day with an un

---

[3]Occupying the same no-man's land of political theory as the "liberal/with it" school of thought.

questioning Pledge of Allegiance to the flag, prime time television was given over to families that were loving, lovable, and complete ("Father Knows Best," "Ozzie and Harriet," "Leave it to Beaver"), schools and colleges were orderly and uncomplicated ("Mr. Peepers," "Halls of Ivy") or even noble and patriotic ("Men of Annapolis"). In fact, this decidedly conservative and conformist generation did not create a drug-ridden youth culture. Drugs and the cultural supports for drug taking that soon followed would alter this generation into what the "conservative/out-of-its" wish to castigate.

Support for the fact that drug use itself, not a more general shift in social attitudes, *is* the problem can be seen in the remarkably uniform ways in which the "drug problem" emerges in "permissive" and "non-permissive" cultures, just as it emerges in a depressingly uniform way in permissive and non-permissive households. And if the availability of drugs to youth and the use of drugs by youth is the "drug problem," then that problem will persist until suppliers and users are confronted and stopped. In nations, in cultures, in treatment centers, in schools where this has been done, there is no longer a drug problem—and whatever underlying problems persist can be addressed for what they are.

In one important sense, however, both the "liberal/with-its" and the "conservative/out-of-its" have an important point. Both see a connection between prevailing social norms and drug use. The "liberals" tend to see drug use as an understandable, even justifiable, reaction to bad social norms, while the "conservatives" see drug use as an inevitable response to pro-drug norms or to the deterioration of anti-drug norms. Holders of either of these views have not been demonstrably effective in curbing drug problems, however, except to the extent they have agreed that drug using is of itself a serious social problem. The social norms—pro and con—which bear on drug use are themselves shaped by drug use. As epidemiologists like Sweden's distinguished Neils Bejerot have pointed out, drug use becomes "epidemic" when the norms which separate a socially outcast minority ("norm breakers") from the larger society ("norm maintainers") are broken down. This can happen in a number of ways. Norm breakers can be attractively publicized (as in sensational publicity given to mass rallies and concerts in which drug use is featured, and to drug-using pop stars, athletes, and other celebrities). As the previously forbidden behavior becomes taken up by former norm-maintainers, the old norms change. Such changes puncture and finally break down the barrier that once held norm-breakers apart from the population at large. This is what happened in the middle 1960s when norm-breaking drug users were perceived as attractive by many of those attending the then burgeoning college campuses. The changed norms on campus quickly spread to all the regions and throughout the social classes serving those campuses—in effect, the society at large—to the extent that anti-drug norms and even some anti-drug laws began to change. In the wake of these changes came a tidal wave of drug-related crime and commerce, an unprecedented rise in youthful chemical dependency, a tenfold increase in adolescent and young adult suicides, a decline in scholastic competence, an emerging failure of school morale (the phenomenon of "teacher burn-out"), and a crisis of confidence in American education.

In the wake of these changes also has come the recurring question, "Is there a drug problem in your school?" The answer is probably "yes." The answer is certainly "yes" if mood-altering chemicals, including alcohol, are playing a part in the maturational or educational development of any students. Fortunately, it is now possible to assert, there are answers beyond "yes."

2.

STEMMING AN EPIDEMIC OF STUDENT DRUG USE: STARTING

It has already been maintained that the "drug problem" cannot begin to be addressed until it is acknowledged as a problem. This, once the denial and defenses fall away, is relatively easy. What happens after that is relatively hard—but well worth the effort. The response to the phenomenon of youthful drug use begins with a conviction—actually a combination of convictions. One has to be convinced that the actions of psychoactive chemicals on the development of children is seriously destructive: a public health problem of the first magnitude. One must be convinced that drugs change children's attitudes, their values, their behavior—and that those changes are not easily correctible, if correctible at all. One must be convinced that drugs can and do addict and kill users, whether directly (as through a fatal dose) or indirectly (as through a car accident or a fall). One must be convinced that drugs work: that the very nicest, strongest, happiest of children, once induced to try drugs, will find them (or some of them) powerfully pleasurable and will want to reproduce the pleasure. One must be convinced that experimentation and "a little" use of drugs is very dangerous; experimentation is the pathway to debilitating use. On the positive side, one must be convinced that the intellectual elegance and the subtleties of perception that result from healthy, drug-free child development are too valuable to pollute or to retard through the action of pleasure-producing chemicals. Finally, and most generally, one must care enough about children—one's own and the mass of them—to take on a considerable burden from which there will be no relief in the immediate future.

Many parents and teachers and increasing numbers of health professionals have taken up the burden, but still greater numbers have not. Serious problems are, as of this writing, unaddressed in whole school districts, whole communities, whole states. Catalysts, a starting point, a blueprint for action are everywhere required. From whence will they come?

Sometimes information alone convinces someone to begin. Nothing pushes aside doubt as knowledge does. There has been an increasing supply of good and challenging material on youth and drugs printed over the past five years. Laying one's hands on it is not always easy. The publishing record of drug-related books and articles tells an interesting story. Commercial (or "trade") publishers have published hundreds of drug-related books, but they are invariably "how-to" manuals, sensational chronicles, or tracts for legalization or for the lifting of anti-drug measures. The anti-drug position has been taken up primarily by small publishers or academic presses or by specific foundations. The volume of anti-drug publishing is comparatively small, but some of it is very well done and is produced by some of the leading thinkers and research scientists in the field. Some worthy examples are the popular and technical books of Dr. Gabriel Nahas (*Keep Off the Grass, Marijuana, The Deceptive Weed,* and others), Helen and Hardin Jones' *Sensual Drugs,* George Russell's careful study of the marijuana controversy, *Marijuana Today,* and the series of monographs published by the American Council for Drug Education on the effects of marijuana, cocaine, and other drugs on the brain, lungs, and other organs.[4] Important studies, including *Drugs and the Nation's High School Students,* already mentioned, can be obtained directly from the National Institute on Drug Abuse in Rockville, Maryland. It is a concern—and really a shame that none of these materials is available in commercial bookstores, but the fact of the matter is that anti-drug sentiment, whatever its extent, is not very well established in the publishing industry.

A good book can spark decisive action, can set a certain type of person in motion. More typically, however, an inspired speaker does the trick: someone who embodies those "convictions" named above, someone whose knowledge about the action of drugs is combined with the requisite affection for children. Such souls are in terrific demand, but they exist. Some are unsung "locals": physicians, counselors, teachers. Some are national authorities and crusaders (up from the ranks of unsung locals) and may include a research psychiatrist, a midwestern school teacher, an Atlanta

[4]Titles of other American Council monographs are appended to this book.

housewife, an officer in the Missouri highway patrol, a Florida pediatrician. Names of especially effective "expert" speakers can be acquired through contacting an extraordinary drug education agency in Atlanta, Georgia: PRIDE (Parent Resources in Drug Education). The PRIDE organization, which has virtually founded a national parents' movement for a drug-free youth, also sponsors a number of yearly conferences for teachers, parents, counselors, and civic leaders in addition to an annual International Conference in the Spring. The "expert" presentations and the dozens of community action workshops at these conferences have been catalytic to beginning effective drug awareness and prevention programs all over the country.

There are better and worse uses of speakers. The better uses are those that will result in continuing, effective action, a restructuring of school, community and, perhaps, household so that the use and exchange of drugs are brought to a halt. This obvious-sounding statement has some very specific implications. The first is that catalytic information—whether from reading material or speakers—should be given to agents of change: to already structured parent organizations, to school staff, to social service agencies, to practicing physicians. The idea is for the effective agents of change in a community to begin behaving differently. The most important people to convince of drug-related losses are those who shape the environment in which children study, mix, and play. Although it is often the first thing a PTA or a school principal thinks of, standing up a "dynamic" drug speaker before a large assembly of students is not a powerful agent of change. This is so for a number of reasons. If the speaker's expertise is medical or scientific, he will lose the less sophisticated thinkers in his audience. He will also lose the student drug users who experiment, in part, because drugs are coming to be regarded as established health hazards—rather in the spirit of the sun-tanned he-man of the billboards and magazine ads who "smokes for taste." The dynamic speaker will also certainly lose the chronic drug-users in his audience: the very target, one might have thought, of his remarks. This happens because health experts who tell the truth about drugs are bearing terrible news to users. In such sessions it is now commonplace to observe users bowing their heads in depression, feigning sleep, or possibly grinning or laughing in uneasy defiance. The latter posture is likely to predominate only when the speaker is poor or unsure of himself; if the speaker is sure and effective, users, in order to maintain their equilibrium, tend to tune out. As drug and alcohol treatment specialists have known for years, a crucial component to drug abuse is denial of a problem. No one is denied more easily than the "outside expert"—unless there is effective and consistent follow-up.

So, there are now some well-documented and persuasive anti-drug materials in print. Some intelligent alarms are being sounded over the air waves. Convincing speakers appear on the stages of the nation's public and private schools. Stimulating conferences are organized. Yet none of these things will in themselves change a community. The job is not done, nor even necessarily started, when the right editorial note is struck, when the "we're sick of drugs!" resolution or city ordinance is passed. In fact, nothing is done until some assignable individual gets busy and behaves differently and begins changing the behavior of others.

It doesn't matter whether the change-maker is a pediatrician, a school administrator, a teacher, or a parent. There are many examples of remarkable achievements from individuals in each of those roles. No special training or expertise is required (although intelligence does not hurt). In fact, a case can easily be made that the most effective change-maker in the drug prevention business has been a non-expert. Mrs. Marsha "Keith" Schuchard, dormant English literature Ph.D. and a suburban Atlanta housewife, was staggered several years ago to observe a birthday cook-out planned for her teenage daughter turn into a formless, furtive evening of drinking and pot smoking. Angry, hurt, and scared, she resolved to act. She called on the parents of every child who attended her "party" and let them know what had happened. While she didn't blame anybody, there was plenty of defensiveness and assertions of "maybe your child, but not my child . . ." Undaunted, Mrs. Schuchard next assembled the parents of the miscreants and provided an opportunity for everybody's anger, hurt, and fear about the climate of their children's socializing to be voiced. This proved a great relief—an occasion even for solidarity and a sense of humor. There was a drug crisis in suburban Atlanta, but at least it was now being acknowledged, the acknowledgement shared, and action planned.

Keith Schuchard is a woman of action. A prototype of what are now called "parent networks" was formed, a voluntary association of parents committed to a drug-free environment for their older children and adolescents. The kids complained, but not very hard, and the parents didn't buckle. Household policies were established—and shared—about hours, about party supervision, about the consequences to follow any incidents of drinking or drug use. In effect, kids were not able to "do it" any more, or at least as easily as they had once done. Moreover, they could no longer claim (truthfully) that "everybody else is 'doing it'." Keith Schuchard's group was named the Nosey Parents Association by critics, and she let that stand. She also forged a cooperative link with middle school and high school staffs and made them allies in the battle for drug-free schools. She badgered the press into investigating and reporting the incidence of drug use and to acknowledge drug-related losses. In the midst of all this, she joined forces with a like-minded professor, Dr. Thomas Gleaton, of Georgia State University, to found first a regional, then a national drug education movement: PRIDE. Finally (and engagingly) she documented what she did and how she did it in a monograph, *Parents, Peers, and Pot,* hundreds of thousands of copies of which have been circulated by the National Institute on Drug Abuse.

Keith Schuchard started, without the aid of organizational supports, with only sketchy information from scientists and health professionals. She was told at every turn and is still told that she is "interfering" with the development of children. She claims otherwise, and with conviction, that, no, traffic in illegal drugs and legal support for drugs (head shops, pro-drug commercial entertainments for youth) have interfered with the development of children, and it is time to stop that. Moreover, it is possible to stop it. She has proved it.

3.

GETTING STARTED IN SCHOOL: FACULTY FIRST

Whether the individual agent of change is a school administrator, an invited "expert," a convinced parent, or an ordinary member of the school staff, the primary group to be addressed is the instructional faculty. The greater the faculty consensus that a drug-free school is desirable and possible, the more effective the school will be in curbing drug use. Faculty, including coaches, ultimately are the eyes and ears of a school's drug prevention program. If they are not alert to possible signs of drug use or if they choose not to respond to them, no amount of care or expertise at "headquarters" can help.

In orienting a faculty to student drug use, some specific expertise is required. Bringing up disciplinary concerns related to drug use is not enough—nor are surveys or estimates that _____% of the student body has tried or uses _____. By themselves, such figures merely generate unease and helplessness. More fundamental—and more effective in converting teachers into change-makers—is a clear explanation of the actions of various drugs on the human system. Many physicians, psychiatrists, and other trained specialists do this very well. Even more fascinating, although trickier to present, are the effects of psychoactive substances on the critical processes undergone by children during periods of rapid growth, including adolescence. Here adolescent psychiatrists and psychologists might be most useful.

Whatever the "source" of expertise, faculty should be reminded that children between the ages of twelve and sixteen are in the period of the most accelerated growth they will ever consciously experience. New size, new potencies, emergent sexuality, emergent capacities for more complicated thought forms are developed during this span of accelerated growth. The growth itself, although age-appropriate and largely welcomed by healthy boys and girls, is the source of strong feelings and new tensions in the growing subject. The adult order expects increased competence and new behaviors from bigger children, and the new expectations create new anxieties. Most school teachers will have little trouble recognizing the standard adolescent adaptations to rapid development: periodic isolation, retreat into intensive peer relationships to the exclusion of family, intense conformity in dress, speech mannerisms, etc. Teachers need to consider the obvious consequences of children's managing these developmental tensions with mood-altering drugs. To the extent drugs ease or replace the age-appropriate tensions, there will be retarded development both into and out of normal adolescence; maturation will be incomplete or may not take place at all.

Those teachers aware of developmental learning theory should be instructed as to the implications of chemicals that break down, distort or slow processes of thought which are in the very process of development. Teachers should, moreover, be cautioned at this point about revising curricula in the direction of less complexity or less rigor in order to accommodate today's "less able" students. In many schools across the country such revisions, like automatic yearly promotions into the next grade level, have served only to accommodate drug use.

In a very important sense academic rigor is a challenge to student drug use. Students pressed to perform at the leading edge of their intellectual range will be unable to do so while taking drugs. Bright students who are not so pressed appear to do well in school, simply because the incorporation and synthesis of new learning—the very reason for school—is not being required of them. Poor curricula and undemanding teachers serve to mask the debilitating effects of student drug use.

Faculty who are made aware of the toxic and developmentally harmful effects of drugs on child development will be less likely to have their heads turned by the standard student pressures on them—and they can be considerable—not to "narc" (confront their drug use). Faculty must also learn to assess student "knowledge" about drugs for what it is: knowledge of drugs, street names, physical characteristics, cost, subjective impressions of taking them. Students "know" that they popped, smoked, inhaled, or drank something and the sensations that followed. Faculty need to know much more. They need to know how seductive pleasure is in building behavior and how destructive toxic chemicals are to learning, to maturation, and to the organs and tissues on which they act.

4.

TRAINING STAFF TO RECOGNIZE AND RESPOND TO STUDENT DRUG USE

Once a school's administration has acknowledged that student drug use is a problem and the school's faculty has been apprised of the personal and scholastic losses inherent to drug use, the school is ready to structure itself to act. Most school teachers do not make vocational plans to be narcotics police or drug counselors, nor should they ever have to include such training in their professional development. However, some teachers and coaches and counselors will most likely be open to taking on specialized training and be willing to meet together as a drug-concerned "Core Group." As few as three or four responsive and committed faculty will serve for even a very large high school or middle school; the more the better. In schools where there is a resident school nurse, he or she should be a member of the Core Group. Core Groups work most effectively when they are led and encouraged by the chief administrative officers in the school (principal, headmaster, etc.).

There are now, as of this writing, intensive workshops to train school staff and others to identify and respond to drug use by the young. Some of these, like the Community Intervention Workshops in Ohio, are intensive five-day sessions, with advanced workshops available afterwards as desired. Staff of many drug treatment centers across the country offer shorter weekend workshops, and they are increasingly willing to come into a school and orient not just a Core Group but the whole faculty to drug-related concerns. And again, the periodic conferences and workshops offered by the PRIDE organization in Atlanta will give school staff who attend not only strategy and technique, but also a community-wide plan for confronting youthful drug use.

THE CORE GROUP

Whatever the "educational" resource selected, a Core Group of committed and well-informed faculty should be formed, procedures established, and meeting times provided for. In order to be effective, Core Group members must be convinced themselves of a few common principles:
— That drug-free youth and a drug-free school are both desirable and possible; that such a position is neither "old fashioned" nor too "idealistic"; that a "little" use or "social use" of drugs is dangerous and unacceptable in healthy child development.
— That drug dependency is a *primary* disease, which will of *itself* cause the deterioration of health, personality, and performance; that ignoring drug use and going after the "underlying problems" of family troubles, peer rejection, etc., will leave the debilitating drug problem intact.
— That drug dependency is a family and social disease: family structure, friendships, even a school community can be fragmented by a single person's drug use.
— That it is imperative to *confront signs of drug use,* even if the confronter has not observed actual drug taking. There are no enduring harms of mistaken concern about a non-user's drug use; there are enduring harms in letting actual drug use go.

On the basis of these shared convictions, the Core Group should make itself, its purpose, and its procedures known to the faculty at large and to the families (not just students, not just parents) served by the school. Core Groups may evolve somewhat different functions at different schools, but at base they should take primary responsibility for:
— *Informing* the faculty at large of the signs of possible student drug use.
— *Establishing procedures* by which faculty who suspect drug use may register that concern to the Core Group and by which the Core Group can collect information about students otherwise suspected of drug use.
— *Maintaining an information pool* of drug-related concerns with inputs from concerned students, parents, and faculty.
— *Contacting parents and school administrators* when a detected drug problem may require treatment or school action.

—*Facilitating referral of students to treatment* when a drug problem is confirmed.
—*Facilitating the student's reentry* into the school program after treatment.
—(Where desired) *Facilitating a student "support group"* to help recovering drug users and others to stay sober.
—*Advising the school administration and faculty on the climate of drug use in the school and making recommendations on drug-related school policy.*

A number of health agencies and drug treatment centers have devised check lists of "danger signs" of student drug use. Sometimes these are printed on slips of paper for faculty to use when they are concerned about a student's possible drug involvement. While the categories on such check lists may be hard to interpret, and while the form-filling process may be a bit tedious and mechanical, this procedure forms a record of concern much more valuable than anecdotal information shared between faculty and Core Group members. In large schools, such a system may be the best and only way to communicate concerns between faculty and Core Group members. Checklists are of course fallible. They can be nonetheless helpful. The best information is that which documents behavior, if possible measurable behavior: i.e., number of absences, number of missing homeworks, number of times unprepared or without necessary classroom materials. The nature of the inappropriate verbal exchange, etc. Since most healthy students are capable on any given day of some form of classroom inappropriateness, provision should be made to record chronic or exceptional instances of problem behavior. In general, helpful comments for drug evaluation record what the teacher sees ("For most of every fifty-minute class last week, Sara put her head down on her desk and appeared to sleep"), not what he or she suspects ("Sara was stoned all week"). Whether through the exchange of checklist information or through otherwise recorded observation, Core Group members should take care to accumulate and monitor the following student developments:

General School Performance

—Distinct *downward* turns in student achievement and performance: good athletes growing lethargic or ineffective, or quitting teams; grades sinking—not just from Cs to Fs, but from As to Bs and Cs.

—Homework not done; unpreparedness for daily discussion and on daily quizzes.
—Lack of feeling or inappropriate feelings expressed about academic reversals.
—Increased absenteeism, chronic absenteeism.
—Increased lateness, chronic lateness.
—Chronic short term illnesses, excuses from class, schedule changes, outside "appointments."
—Diminished extracurricular involvement, unreliability in group commitments.

Physical Signs

—Loss of coordination.
—Dazed lapses in speech and movement.
—Bloodshot or glassy eyes (or eyes hidden with dark glasses).
—Chronic protestation of feeling ill.
—Chronic injuries.
—Slurred speech, incoherent speech.
—Poor hygiene, indifference to poor hygiene.

Other Behavior

—Possession of drug-related paraphernalia.
—Possession of drugs (claimed always to be somebody else's).
—Possession of large amounts of money.
—Chronic routine rules violations.
—Extreme discomfort/hostility in discussing drug use, drug-related issues.
—Inappropriate anger, vulgarity.
—Chronic dishonesty (lying, academic cheating and short cuts).
—Smelling of drink or drugs, smelling of incense or other "cover-up" scents.
—Conversation, joking preoccupied with drugs.

One or more of these signs may be inaccurately reported by a faculty member, or they may be reported accurately but be unrelated to drug use. Core members are well aware of this and are looking for confirmation, for multiple indications of a drug-linked behavior. Their records are kept and dated, not for general student reporting or for discipline, but strictly as a gauge of possible drug problems. By no means does collecting such information preclude direct, caring confrontations between classroom teachers and students. The more direct confrontation the better; but if concern is being registered by a number of different teachers in isolation of one another, diagnosis of a serious problem could be delayed.

When there is a clear indication of possible drug-related behavior, a Core Group member should arrange to see the student in question. The student should be told that he or she is in no special disciplinary trouble, but there are some school concerns that need to be shared. A model expression of those concerns might go as follows:

Core Group Member: Ted, thanks for coming in. This is not a disciplinary meeting. You're not in trouble. We are concerned, though, about your performance recently. We are especially concerned about your slip in biology and math and your incompleted papers in English. You have been absent quite a bit, too. What is happening?

Ted: (responds)

Core Group: You say there have been a lot of hassles at home and you haven't been feeling too well this spring. Can you tell me about the hassles? What kinds of sickness have you had?

Ted: (responds)

Core Group: What are you planning to do about these low grades, missing homework, and the late papers? Do you think you can turn your slump around?

Ted: (responds)

Core Group: Good, we hope you do. One of the things we look for these days when a good student like you starts to miss school and fall behind in his work is the possibility of drug use. If you were into drugs, this kind of school performance would make sense. Have you been involved in any drug use?

Ted: (responds)

Core Group: We have no evidence that you have been involved, but we have learned to ask. We'll take your word for it, Ted. But let's get together again at the end of the marking period and review your performance. Our understanding is that there will be no more missing homework in math, no more napping in biology, and no more missed deadlines in English. Agreed?

Ted: (responds)
Core Group: Fine, if we don't see any changes, we'll have to try again, until we get to whatever the problem is. Once again, thanks for coming in.

Following such an interview, it is always a good idea to phone the student's parents—or have them come into school—to share the school's concerns and to hear what they are seeing at home which might help explain the problem behavior. As in the meeting with the student, only the possibility of drug use need be raised— "We have learned to ask." Sometimes doing so strikes a chord and parents are relieved to have an outlet for their own fears and observations. Even if parents seem uninterested, unduly frightened, or defensive, it is still appropriate to raise the question. Once again, no harm comes from a groundless concern expressed about drug use; great harm can result from failing to pursue a concern.

If the problem behaviors persist and/or there is new and more substantial indication of drug involvement, a second student-parent conference might result in a recommended or required outside assessment of the suspected drug use. These are routinely and increasingly skillfully done at drug treatment centers (some attached to hospitals, some not) throughout the country. Sometimes pediatricians and other physicians are informed and trained to do drug use assessments. Physicians and treatment centers that have access to some of the new urine testing devices for marijuana use are often effective where others are not; oral interviews and standard physical examinations are sometimes insufficient to detect a skillfully evasive early drug user.

If an outside assessment indicates some drug use, or if Core Group conferences determine some drug use, the Core Group and the student may compose a written "contract" according to which, over a specified period of time (six weeks is a recommended minimum), the student will agree to use no drugs or alcohol. "No-use" contracts may also stipulate other behaviors inside and outside of school: curfew hours, numbers of nights out per week, homework times, etc. Parents may also be party to contracts. A contract can be helpful both as a straightforward curb on drug use and as a diagnostic aid. Keeping a contract can be an important first step in a student's becoming drug free; this is especially likely if a student's teachers, advisors, and parents support him and praise positive increments of change during the contract period. If the student *fails* to keep the contract, this is important information: a school-aged youth *unable* to refrain from alcohol and drugs for six weeks may be drug-dependent. The consequences for breaking a contract should always be established in advance. Where there is good reason to suspect that a student's drug use is advanced, it is recommended that the consequences for breaking a contract be (1) that the student have a professional assessment at once and not be readmitted into the school's program until there is written notification that he or she is drug free and (2) that a student make a new "no-use" contract that will extend for the duration of his or her time in school. If these standards and contracts are not kept, the student should be referred to drug treatment and readmitted to the school only upon successful completion of the treatment (discussed further in REFERRAL FOR TREATMENT).

When a student is observed or caught visibly intoxicated at school or in possession of drugs or exchanging them, the process is much more direct. Such students, if they are badly intoxicated, should be taken at once to the nurse or other designated administrative officer. There they should be kept quiet until their parents can come to take them home. At that point, if the student is coherent, he should be advised of what he had done and the rule violated (see DISCIPLINE AND SCHOOL POLICY); if the student is not coherent, he should be apprised of his offense the next day—but not allowed to attend ordinary classes. Students caught under the influence of drugs or using or exchanging them at school should not be readmitted without an outside assessment indicating that the student is drug free and/or, in the case of drug selling, will not pose a danger to other students in the school. Students who cannot be so assessed should be referred to drug treatment until they can be. If treatment is refused by either the student or family, the student should be expelled forthwith. If, as in some states, expulsion is not possible under the laws regulating schools, the student may be remanded to a program of home study until the school's terms are met.

The faculty Core Group should take on the responsibility of contacting and getting to know informed physicians[5] and drug treatment facilities in the area served by the school so that they can refer families for help when a child is in trouble. Where no such professional supports exist, Core Group and parent organizations (see PARENT AWARENESS NETWORK) should work to establish

---

[5] It is still the case that many physicians, including pediatricians, have little interest in or knowledge about the effects of drugs available to youth.

them. While some children may experiment with some drugs and then discontinue further involvement, students are typically not able to stop chronic use voluntarily; they don't "grow out of it." Without treatment, drug abuse progresses in the direction of antisocial behavior, physical illness and death.

Perhaps the greatest service a Core Group could provide to their faculty colleagues and to the student and parent bodies they serve is to instruct them about the progressive nature of drug abuse. Students, parents, and teachers alike should be made aware that there is no "safe" level of drug use for developing children. The staffs of the most longstanding treatment centers have now outlined with some precision the stages of drug use that lead to dependency and illness:

1. *Experimentation:* Through peer or sibling inducement, a child tries an available mind-altering chemical—e.g., a prescription pill, marijuana, alcohol—and, perhaps after an initial failure or two, succeeds in getting high. If he feels good as a result, he has *learned to mood swing.* If there are no adverse consequences (vomiting, getting caught and punished), the child is likely to try to repeat the experience.
2. *Casual or Social Use:* Whether through clandestine get-togethers with friends or at poorly supervised or unsupervised "parties,"[6] or occasionally in solitude, children *plan for* opportunities to get high. They are now *seeking the mood swing.* In this stage, users will begin to buy some of the preferred illegal substance for themselves. The arrangements to do so will be furtive. Lies will be told, phone conversations become cryptic or truncated. There may be irregular money dealings. Peer friendships rearrange themselves, with drug-using friends replacing "straight" friends to the point that the latter are excluded altogether.
3. *Chronic Use:* Drug use has now become the central, governing activity of the user. High commitment activities and obligations are abandoned, or performance becomes erratic in them. Discipline problems, often relating to negligence or truancy, arise at school. Users are often "caught" using or possessing drugs at this stage and will characteristically deny serious involvement. *Nothing* will arouse stronger feelings than confronting a user at this stage.

[6] The word "party" has been appropriated by the current generation of children and young adults as a euphemism for intoxication.

The family—all members—may be divided in their response to the user; camps of supporters/enablers will oppose camps of prosecutors/punishers. Family disruption will be *serious and painful.* Unless there is an intervention, users often leave home or are ordered out of the house in anger. The user, unaided, will now seek to *maintain the mood swing.* He will no longer experience as much elation in drug taking, but will seek to counteract feeling ill and anxious: he is taking drugs at this point to feel "normal." Defiance and expressed anger will often match feelings, when the user is sober, of profound worthlessness and shame. Untreated, the user at this stage is likely to put himself or herself in a life threatening situation, to be jailed or otherwise institutionalized, or to become seriously ill. Should a chronic user be treated and begin the process of recovery, he or she will not be able to drink or use drugs again on a "social" pattern.

Because not all children who experiment with drugs go on to become dependent on them, pro-drug spokesmen[7] like to argue that marijuana, alcohol, and other "first-use" drugs are not "threshold" drugs to more serious involvement. Such arguments are misleading. First, they ignore the losses to users—in personality and in learning—before the dependency stage. Secondly, they do not address the indisputable fact that problem users always and only began as experimenters with what they were led to believe were controllable drugs: most typically, cigarettes, alcohol, and marijuana. Whoever may make the case that less potent drugs are not stepping stones to more potent ones, recovering addicts are never among them. An indisputable maxim in the face of present findings on drug use is that the surest way to curb youthful drug dependency is to alter the social climate where youthful drug experimentation is the norm and to eliminate so far as possible the practical opportunities for children to experiment with drugs.

---

[7]Examples are national lobbying organizations like NORML and the several wide-circulation magazines which, like *High Times,* are given over exclusively to promoting drug use for the young.

5.

ESTABLISHING A SCHOOL-FAMILY PARTNERSHIP IN TREATING DRUG CONCERNS

School staff, whether Core Group members or otherwise, should work as closely as they can with families of students in trouble. For a variety of reasons, school staff are often reluctant to do this. The chief reason for the reluctance is not usually articulated openly, but it should be: confronting drug use involves bad feelings in all parties.

Once again, the school person confronting the student entertains a complex of unpleasant feelings. Consciously, he or she may have serious reservations about intruding into the world of the student's "private" choices and most intimate feelings; talking to children about drugs can be as awkward as talking to them about sex—and for the same reasons. Moreover, one cannot tell what a student's response will be in a drug-related confrontation. Feelings of anger and rejection are common. For some teachers the inherently adversarial dimension of the teacher-student relationship cannot withstand an extra increment of tension. Teachers also frequently express a "this is not my job" response, a claim with some substance to it. Then there is the nagging realization that one may himself or herself have a drink or two in the evening after school, may have tried pot and other drugs; if so, one tends to doubt one's authority and effectiveness in confronting student drug use.

When a factor of parental anger or defensiveness—or perhaps a threatened lawsuit—is added, a teacher's inclination to pursue a drug concern diminishes powerfully. Nevertheless, despite some dramatic examples to the contrary, parents are far more likely to be allies than enemies of school staff responding to drug concerns.

In fact, faculty dread of bearing troubling news to parents is usually not borne out by the actual response of parents. What school staff can forget is that the behavior causing a problem in school is very likely observable, perhaps exaggeratedly so, at home. School concerns very often serve to confirm parental concerns and can on that account be a great boost to effective action. Parent defensiveness can also be avoided by adopting a non-accusing tone. Just as in the optimal home-school relationship parents should feel free to identify health and development problems of their children to school officials, school staff should feel free to do the same. As in the Core Group meetings with students, problem behaviors, as closely observed as possible, should be shared with parents. Drug use need only be *raised* as one possible explanation for the problem behavior: "We have learned to ask." Even when drug involvement is substantial and the problem is serious, school officials should adhere as strictly as they can to the posture of helper, as opposed to prosecutor. This does not mean that school rules and policies indicating dismissal or suspension for drug offenses should be softened to accommodate bad parent or student feeling. Teachers must hold fast to the conviction that school discipline, including expulsion, for drug involvement is a consequence of drug use, not of unfeeling administration.

Core Group members must continually remind each other that a groundless concern about drug use, professionally and humanely expressed, does no substantial harm. A case simply cannot be made today that there is in any sphere of American life an excessive concern about youthful drug use. This could conceivably happen in the future, although it seems a rather remote possibility; what we have in the interim is an epidemic of drug abuse among the young.

So long as that is the case, two-way lines of communication between the school (particularly the Core Group) and school families, should be clearly established and utilized. School-to-family mailings and open parent forums should establish the school's drug *policy,* from the Core Group procedures already discussed to the school's disciplinary procedures with respect to drug use. Many schools have reported encouraging results from inviting parents (see PARENTS AWARENESS NETWORK) to register concerns about any student's drinking or drug-taking to the Core Group at school. A potentially "Big Brother" aspect of this system seems not to be a discouraging factor, once the health-promoting, non-disciplinary nature of the Core Group's business is clearly communicated to parents. One thing which is best made very clear in all school-family communications about drugs is that classroom concerns, Core Group concerns, and parent-registered concerns do not become part of a student's "permanent record" or file. Core Group information should be made readily available both to parents and students on request, although the anonymity of the information's source should be respected if requested.

The aim, finally, is for school staff, students, and parents to share a common understanding of school rules and school procedures when student drug involvement is suspected or detected. At best, every drug-related confrontation in a classroom, in the Core Group, or in a disciplinary action should be communicated thoroughly and speedily to parents. And where school size and facilities permit (most small schools and nearly all independent day and boarding schools are well set up for this), the students should be apprised at once and in detail about serious school actions—dismissals, referrals to treatment—stemming from drug use. Schools and families should learn to rely on each other for sharp observation, for help, and for action.

6.

REFERRAL TO TREATMENT

At what point does a student have a "drug problem"? At what point is a girl or boy no longer able to live his or her life without the use of alcohol or drugs? The clearest sign is when use has been detected repeatedly, in the face of strict prohibitions. Children showing one or more of the signs of Stage Three involvement (see p. 22) almost certainly are in trouble. The school psychologist at Deerfield Academy offers an interesting litmus: "When a student is caught with drugs, that is a good indication that drug use may be advanced." A question commonly put to users by drug treatment specialists is "Have drugs caused you any problems in your life?" "Problems" can include auto accidents, deteriorating parent relationships (regardless to whom the user assigns blame), declining school performance, run-ins with school authorities and police, rejection of former friends. If the user answers in the affirmative, there is a drug problem.

To determine whether a child needs specialized treatment, a professional "assessment" should be made either by an informed physician or by a drug treatment center. The object of an assessment is to determine the present level of a user's involvement. If use-level is not too far advanced, a non-use "contract" (see discussion, p. 20) may be proposed, possibly supplemented by a weekly group session with other young people with similar diagnoses. Whether the user's family or school initiates the assessment, both should be informed of the outcome.

If the assessment indicates a possibility of drug dependence (Stage Three), then an "evaluation" in a drug treatment program or center should be considered. Sometimes initial evaluations are preceded by an *intervention,* a confrontation between the user, his or her family, school staff, and others well acquainted with the user and concerned about his or her drug use. The intervention sessions, moderated by a professional facilitator, are structured so that the user hears a consecutive series of statements by those closest to him documenting his drug use and drug-related behavior. Participants are asked to stress how the user's behavior has affected their lives and made them feel. Users also hear each participant express concern and affection for them. Interventions are especially valuable when (1) the user is reluctant to enter treatment and/or (2) the user has reached an age (eighteen years old or older) at which he cannot be treated against his will. Interventions are dramatic and invariably emotional; in a controlled setting the user must hear at length what he or she has refused to hear during his active drug involvement. Skillfully conducted, an intervention can lead to a genuine self-evaluation on the user's part, a crucial prerequisite for successful treatment.

In the typical inpatient treatment format, the "evaluation" period lasts for a week or a little longer. During this time the user is closely monitored and is kept on a tight schedule of presentations, examinations, and small group sessions. Critical to the evaluation period is that detoxification—the clearing of the user's system of drugs—takes place. Patients are kept strictly drug free, at most centers free even of prescription sedatives. Although painful or dangerous withdrawal is unlikely, medical support is available. Besides detoxification, patients in evaluation are often required to compose a complete personal "drug history" from first use to the present. Patients farther along in treatment and trained staff members work intensively with new patients to insure the drug history's honesty; typically early versions are incomplete, the whole story rarely told at the outset. Typically also the patient's resolve to "stonewall" the treatment—"tell them what they want to hear"—until he or she is back on the street. When insincerity, hostility, or incomplete disclosure is challenged in the course of the evaluation week—which it invariably is—strong feelings of anger and fear are expressed, and the staff are trained to point out to users the connections between these feelings and drug use. When detoxification, medical and psychological examinations, and the patient's "drug history" have been completed, the user and his family (and perhaps other members of the intervention group) are assembled again. At this session the user shares his or her drug history with his family, and makes a determination of whether or not he believes he is chemically dependent. The treatment staff have also made a determination, but the important decision from the standpoint of treatment is the patient's. Formal *inpatient treatment,* a four to six week program to follow, usually is undertaken voluntarily. Patients are advised that treatment is demanding, that they will be tempted to drop out of it and run away, and that it is possible to do so. The decision to remain in treatment may be influenced significantly by consequences set by the family for failing to do so, by the school which may make successful completion of treatment and a satisfactory recommendation from it a condition of readmission, and also by the courts for youngsters arrested for drug-related offenses.

The treatment program for chemical dependency *is* demanding. There are a densely packed series of individual therapy sessions, professionally facilitated family sessions, group sessions, and carefully selected films and outside presentations. A little school work and free time for exercise and relaxation are factored in, but the principal agenda is the treatment program. As the patient becomes increasingly drug-free and clear-headed, strong feelings of guilt and shame and worthlessness come to the surface as, often for the first time, the implications of one's drug use are considered by an unclouded consciousness. Here again the staff recognizes and even encourages the expression of these feelings. Once they are acknowledged and experienced for what they are the user can begin the constructive business of managing and channeling them in ways that do not require drugs or alcohol. Successful treatment teaches users that they need help and practices them in using, getting, and giving help. This is the most durable lesson when the formal treatment program is over.

The foregoing description of inpatient drug dependence treatment has been called the Minnesota Model since it was pioneered in the state that developed the term "chemical dependence." Minnesota has often been in the forefront of human services programs. The sophistication of their inpatient chemical dependence treatment is the result of a unique state law requiring that all health insurance plans provide for at least 28 days of inpatient chemical dependent treatment. This Minnesota approach, usually involving aftercare using Alcoholics Anonymous and/or Narcotics Anonymous is rapidly becoming common throughout the nation. Other inpatient and quasi-inpatient models have been developed with many similar features, some lasting for as long as one year. These longer programs generally include return to school during treatment. All programs mandate regular family involvement, especially for teenage chemical dependence patients.

In addition to these inpatient models, a variety of outpatient approaches to teenage drug dependence have been developed in recent years. These are less easily categorized but most include family involvement, positive peer support and, when necessary, confrontation. Many use urine testing to insure drug free participation. All these approaches, whether inpatient or outpatient, owe much to the wisdom of the Alcoholics Anonymous program. They are also all tough, demanding complete abstinence from all intoxicating drug use, including alcohol use.

One caution before the discussion moves on to the reintegration of the "recovering" user into school life. While chemical dependency treatment programs vary in substance and structure, the most well established ones, those based on the so-called "Minnesota plan" (described above), are more similar than they are different. Some adolescents remain drug free after treatment; others manage to do it only after being "recycled" through treatment, while still others never make it. This should not cloud the fact that, compared to any known alternative, treatment is the best bet for converting a drug-dependent child into a drug-free child. The alternative many families adopt, because it seems less dramatic and can be kept more private, is individualized psychotherapy with a social worker, psychologist or psychiatrist. There is a growing consensus across the country among those involved in drug abuse prevention that individual therapy is a relatively unproductive approach to youthful drug problems. Psychology is less uniform in its application than dentistry. There are a wide variety of assumptions, including contradictory ones, underlying current psychological practice. Moreover, many psychological models of cure require (and rightly so) sobriety as a condition of carrying on therapy. Yet many young drug users find it relatively easy to undergo regular therapy sessions without in any way altering their pattern of drug use. As one former drug-using student told the writer:

> I went through three years of talk therapy—and was hospitalized twice—without having to change my drinking and drugging. I used to go high to my psychologist's office. Whenever I'd get fixed up with a new shrink, my first concern was always, "Is this guy going to stop me

from using or not?" Not until AA got hold of me and confronted my drinking did I even begin to change.

Recovery from drug abuse does not begin until a user is detoxified. Most psychologists and psychiatrists do not require it, nor are they equipped to monitor it. While informed psychiatrists and psychologists can be invaluable in assessing drug problems (see USING COMMUNITY RESOURCES) and for help in referring students to treatment, their involvement with drug-using students cannot be assumed by either parents or schools or "take care of" the problem.

One overriding principle must be grasped. The teenager's drug use is the responsibility of the teenager *and* the concerned adults in his or her life. These adults must make clear that NO USE of intoxicating drugs will be tolerated and that actions to achieve this goal will be based on the principle of "Doing Whatever Is Necessary." Thus an initial effort might be simple, clear parental and school limit setting, often with regular urine testing to insure that the teenager is truly drug free. If this fails, then the response is escalated, perhaps to an outpatient chemical dependence program. Later, an inpatient program may be required. Still later involuntary treatment under court order may be necessary.

Most children, many with severe drug problems, can be stopped and returned to health by undramatic interventions once the child knows the adults are serious. On the other hand, some youth—even in early stages of drug use—require the full range of treatment services before they are able to remain drug free. The point is that the child needs to know the responsible adults—especially the parents—will "Do Whatever Is Necessary" to help the child grow up healthy and drug free.

Throughout this process the concerned adults must not simply assume that treatment means the youth is being monitored for drug use or that his or her drug use is even being dealt with since some therapists and more than a few drug treatment programs have a mistakenly tolerant attitude toward some drug use—particularly marijuana and alcohol use. It is important for adults to assess the attitudes and performance of treatment programs, and to remember that the responsibility for the care of the child remains theirs in or out of treatment.

7.

REINCORPORATING RECOVERING USERS

Students emerging drug free after residential treatment face a number of challenges, some of them obvious, others not easily understood by those not involved in treatment. The external controls on drug supply and the professional and peer support for staying drug free are cut back dramatically when a user leaves treatment. For this reason, most treatment programs specify a period of aftercare during which, from several weeks to a year, students may keep a modified schedule of school courses and then report to group sessions consisting of other former users. In these sessions, group members share general frustrations and difficulties in staying drug free. Aftercare is typically supplemented by attendance at one or more weekly Alcoholics Anonymous meetings. Patients leaving treatment also often make home/school contracts specifying behaviors and performance levels to be achieved and activities, including drug use, to be avoided. Readmission to school should be contingent on strict adherence to the student's contract as monitored by the school's Core Group. Many treatment centers build into a "graduate's" contract a strict buffer period of up to six weeks during which they may not contact or speak to former drug-using friends. This is an important stricture, as "using" friends are part of the recovering patient's "euphoric recollection"—and are powerful lures to drug use. Moreover, the recovering user is a serious threat to the continuing user, and the latter often feels compelled to undermine (and therefore dismiss) the recovering user's treatment.

Many schools have formed support groups to ease the reentry of recovering drug users and to help them remain drug free. Support groups may meet before, during, or after school hours and should be facilitated by a Core Group member. School psychologists and others certified in guidance are often trained to run such groups, and non-professionals can be trained in relatively brief workshops to do so. The purpose of the support group is to help members maintain sobriety. The group leader is "nondirective" in that he or she does not determine the agenda of the session, nor does he or she advise or instruct members what to do except that drug use is not acceptable. As in treatment, the expression of personal feelings is encouraged, so that appropriate, drug-free outlets for them can be discussed. Like many continuing, process-oriented groups, the support group is more or less openly structured.

Support group sessions usually begin with "open time" during which any member may express something important that he or she is feeling at the moment. After this, students may share difficulties they are having in managing their school, out-of-school, and home life as they try to stay drug free. Also, members' responses to each other, even critical ones, are encouraged and discussed: e.g., "I don't like the way Al laughs at what people say, even when there's no humor in it" or "Jenny, I don't feel you are taking the rest of us very seriously." Around vacation times or prom season, facilitators may want to focus group discussion on how, specifically, members are going to plan their time with a different routine facing them, including circumstances in which members are likely to have to make a decision on drinking and drug use. At these times, facilitators may ask members very basic questions: "What will you say, John, when your date asks to stop by a keg party after the dance?" "How are you going to respond when you see your old using friends at a party?"

Three general ground rules apply in all support group sessions. (1) *One person at a time*. Participants are encouraged to speak without interruption until they are finished. (2) *Confidentiality*. Group members agree that whatever is said in group sessions not be shared or used in other settings. (3) *No "killer" statements*. While direct confrontation and critical comments and questions are encouraged, all participants are asked to state their position in a form that is constructive to those to whom it is addressed: i.e., "I don't agree with that" or "I don't see it that way" is fine; "That's ridiculous" or "You don't know what you're talking about" is not.

Finally, although it is important that they keep some distance from the rest of the school community while they are in session, support groups may want to meet openly about their aims and procedures with the student body at large and with the faculty. Otherwise, considerable confusion and even resentment can fester about what may appear to be "special treatment for the druggy kids." Support groups may constitute "special treatment," but it comes at no one else's expense, and it may be crucial to the health and development of group members.

8.

RULES AND DISCIPLINE: SHAPING THE CLIMATE OF CONSEQUENCES IN WHICH STUDENTS DECIDE ON DRUG USE

A child's first decision to use or to decline use of an illegal drug typically occurs between his twelfth and sixteenth years—between sixth grade and the junior year in high school. There are of course exceptions on either side of that time slot, but it will suffice as a reliable current guideline for parents and school staff. Developmental psychologists have determined that children do not typically make such choices on the basis of abstract moral principles. Rather, they make them on the basis of perceived consequences of their actions. The information that shapes these perceptions is the single greatest influence on a child's decision to use drugs. Health dangers that are real, but which are too complicated or hazily communicated to youth, will not deter drug use. Laws and school rules forbidding use *will* deter use, provided they are clearly and frequently communicated to students and students can see them in operation as they are enforced.

The United States is undergoing a period in which youthful drug use is epidemic. Drug use by the young constitutes a public health concern of the first order. In addition, the epidemic is supported by a massive and socially corrosive network of criminal and technically legal drug dealing and promotion. Drug use has contributed nothing positive to the culture of youth, and it takes a continuing toll in youthful productivity, learning, and health. Therefore the schools' rules about the use and exchange of drugs should be as strict as state regulations allow and as practical as enforcement procedures permit. The best and most deterrent school policy is that students who possess, use, or exchange drugs at school or at school-related activities should be removed from the school at once and readmitted after a specified period of time only when, in the case of dependency, they have successfully completed a school-approved program of drug treatment or, if dependency is not established, a professional assessment is made and a no-use contract is agreed upon by the student and his family. In neither case should the school readmit a student without an acceptable student commitment (contract) to remain drug free. When such a commitment is not or cannot be made, the student should not be readmitted to the school. If a commitment is made and broken, then that student should likewise be dismissed from the school.

Public and private schools differ in their ability to dismiss students. Public schools are regulated by statutory law and may not suspend or dismiss students from school unless court and statute-dictated "due process" is given and the delinquent student can be demonstrated to present a danger to other students and to the educational process. Chronic drug users and drug dealers can be regarded as constituting such a danger. If they are given a school hearing in which the complaint against them is made clear, they can be sent home, referred for an assessment or for treatment, and can, if they are repeat offenders, be separated from the school permanently. Some public schools have established an isolated "in-house suspension" or "tank" for chronic truants and drug offenders. Students of this status show up at school to a room monitored by school staff and isolated from the rest of the school. Assignments are given and their completion is monitored by specially designated teachers. Tutoring is sometimes available. Students who disrupt or fail to attend in-house suspension sessions may be dismissed permanently from the school.

Private schools and their clients are, by contrast, bound by contract law rather than statutory law and, consequently, have much more latitude and discretion in removing problem students from school. Contract law, in essence, binds a school to do what it says it does in its stated policies and in the enrollment agreements sent to parents. Private schools therefore are in a favorable position to take a strong stated stand against drug use and to act on it. Nevertheless, only a small minority of private schools do this. Some school administrators balk at the inflexibility of an automatic dismissal policy for "first offenses." Other, less well-established private schools may, literally, be unable to afford the loss of tuitions such a policy would entail. Ultimately, the kind of disciplinary policy the school adopts reflects its consensus about the magnitude and seriousness of drug and alcohol use by school-aged children.

Again, as of this writing, the great majority of private schools have adopted what is in effect a "second chance policy." In other words, a student caught smoking pot in his room (in boarding schools) or elsewhere on the campus would be brought up before the student or administrative judiciary committee and given "serious" punishment of some kind: a suspension, a probationary status, a penitential work detail. A second offense or, as some schools put it, "repeated offenses," may result in dismissal. "Second chance" policies have the advantage of flexibility and hold out the possibility of reform-without-banishment. They also seem to lighten or at least delay the inevitable student and parent storms which often accompany dismissal decisions. Unfortunately, there is every indication that such policies not only fail to reduce the incidence of drug use in the school, they seem positively to support it. This is fairly easy to understand if one considers the decision-making process of actual adolescents. Drug-taking decisions can be very impulsive. The setting for the decision is invariably clandestine and furtive: both novices and seasoned users know they are breaking rules. Considerable face can be lost if someone declines an offer of an illegal drug. In the best of circumstances, a student on the brink of deciding to use or to decline a drug should not have to summon up elaborate moral and biomedical arguments; he should be able, credibly, to point to the certainty of his dismissal if he is detected, to the home trouble that would follow, etc., and say, "Are you kidding?" or perhaps just, "No thanks." A no-second-chance drug policy encourages such responses. It is obvious, but nonetheless important to stress, that a child who knows he will be "in trouble" but not "kicked out" if he uses a drug is apt to make different decisions than he would if he is certain he will be "kicked out." The stricter policy helps maintain a barrier between users and non-users. Moreover, the dismissal-for-first-use policy has led, in schools that have adopted it, to fewer drug-related incidents and to fewer dismissals. Strict rules strictly enforced decrease the incidence of drug use in a school. Combined with the other school measures discussed, they can eliminate drug use altogether.

In some ways draconian rules about student drug use may seem at odds with the previous discussion of the concern and support given to suspected users and to recovering users. Is it being recommended here that drug-involved students be alternately coddled and throttled? No. Many school staffs have proved that strict school prohibitions on drink and drugs are not incompatible with a caring, therapeutic approach to students in trouble. It should never be a disciplinary offense to confess voluntarily or otherwise to discuss one's own or somebody else's drug use with a school counselor or Core Group member. Students seeking and needing help should be able to get it from trained school staff without fear of disciplinary reprisals. At the same time school staff who work with drug-involved students must make it plain to those students that they are obligated by the same rules as any other student, and that the counselors themselves will see to it that the rules are enforced. This is an important point. School counselors must have room to maintain confidences and to discuss a student's previous drug use, even if it has been in violation of school policy. Counselors, however, should not accept or support current drug use. Accepting, even tacitly, ongoing drug use on a student's part helps to reinforce that use. Strict rules against drug use, rehabilitation of former drug users, and humane counseling of experimental and occasional users can be mutually enhancing dimensions of a school's drug awareness program—provided that current drug use is always confronted and, to the best of counselors' abilities, stopped.

One of the thorniest problems that schools face—at least day schools—is the application of their drug policies outside school grounds and outside school hours. Very clearly a school's concern about a student's drug taking does not stop when he or she leaves the campus and crosses the street. Nor, given the storage and action of drugs on the human system, are the *effects* of drugs taken outside of school unrelated to school performance and behavior. But the fact of the matter is that public and private day schools cannot and should not serve *in loco parentis* outside the school. It is both futile and demoralizing for a school to attempt to hold students accountable for behaviors the school cannot possibly monitor. This does not mean, however, that there must forever be a "gap" between what schools teach and do about drug use and what students do "after school."

The national parents' movement, now flourishing in several regions of the country, has evolved to fill the gap (see FORMING A PARENTS AWARENESS NETWORK). Parents who share the school's commitment to drug-free youth and who take the time to organize and share a few simple procedures will make a profound impact on their children. As will be discussed more fully in a section to follow, a parents' network need not have one hundred percent membership and cooperation, or even a majority, to begin to be effective in changing the climate of youthful drug use. It is possible even to imagine a day when schools, families and community (police, merchants, government, etc.) will work in concert to promote drug-free youth, although this is far from the case at present.

Once again private schools, which have more discretion in dismissing students and which may legally require specific behaviors, dress, and other special conditions of enrollment, usually have more leverage—if they choose to apply it—with their parent bodies than public schools do. Before the middle Sixties, when casual drinking was not a norm at preteen "parties" onward, several headmasters and headmistresses adopted a policy of dismissing students known to have been drinking during vacations, even if in the company of their parents. The advantage of such a policy is that students are spared the confusion and extra tension of moving between one decision-making climate and another. Another advantage is that ambivalent or uninformed parents may be prodded by such a policy into making clearer, more effective family policies on drink and drug use. Families who resent the prod, who see no problem, or who have opposing views on drink and drug use by school-aged children have recourse to other schools. The continuing problem, however, with "anywhere, any time" rules is that they can and will be violated without detection, and this creates an anxious climate among the student body. Students and parents both become reluctant to talk about actual drinking and drug use, including serious problems. The most promising general policy, then, is a strict "no-use," first-time dismissal (or referral) policy at school, bolstered by a "no-use" policy at home, with clear consequences established for violations. This policy should stand until the youth has reached a legal age of informed consent and/or as long as he is a member of an institution that makes such requirements.

Is such a policy, in its actual application, unfeeling? Does expelling drug users immediately or ultimately really solve any problems, or is this just a way of passing them on to resourceless parents and the community at large? Both questions are fair, but the answer to each is an emphatic no. A policy is not unfeeling simply because it raises bad feelings in those affected by it. A school which promises to dismiss students for drug use and which keeps that promise does two important things for the health and welfare of students. It puts up a formidable barrier to experimentation and casual use of dangerous drugs. It also presents violators and their families with a dramatic and serious consequence of drug use. Up to the present historical moment, schools, either through inaction or through "second chance" policies, have accommodated and thus unintentionally promoted student drug use.

Dismissal from school and/or placement in an intensive drug treatment program is a dramatic consequence. Dramatic consequences are more likely to stimulate important behavioral change than are either advice or accommodation. Alcoholics Anonymous organizations have reported for years what drug treatment staffs have now confirmed: that until users are able to experience significant negative consequences of drink or drug use, they are unlikely to recover.

Is interrupting or terminating school membership the right negative consequence? For users it very often is, and for non-users it very definitely is. Against the prospect of a drug-free learning environment, the separation (temporarily or permanently) of users from school is a very limited harm, if a harm at all. Experimenters or casual users who are caught and disciplined need not terminate, or even interrupt, their education. Movement, after a drug incident, from private into public or from public into private schools is common—and often catalytic to positive change. But again, such a change unaccompanied by a thoroughgoing drug assessment and well developed "no use" contract from the student is a chancey prospect. Chronic users who are caught and disciplined do not lose valuable educational opportunity; they have been poor subjects for educational opportunity since their drug use commenced, and the greatest educational boost they could receive is the cessation of their drug use. Drug-using students may attend school (although they are notorious truants) during periods of chronic use, but their accrued education while they are doing so is usually negligible.

Moreover, policymakers should be aware that the educational losses brought about through the drug use of some students extend well beyond the users themselves. The atmosphere of a classroom of thirty students is profoundly affected by the passive or irritable presence of even a small number of students who are either under the influence of drugs or who are unable to engage in classroom business because of prior intoxication. From a classroom teacher's perspective, nothing dampens the learning climate like passivity and non-engagement. Students do not feel intellectual enthusiasm, nor, often, can they even feign it, when they are aware of drug-altered classmates. The situation can be likened to the difficulty one may have maintaining a focused conversation with a seat mate on a bus when someone nearby is unconscious or babbling incoherently.

Students whose drug use has made them passive, hostile, or unprepared for schoolwork also diminish the effectiveness of their teachers. Teachers, like students, perform along a range of enthusiasm and effectiveness. Eager, responsive students encourage teachers to perform at the top of their ranges; unresponsive students shut teachers down. Passivity and incapacity often appear to teachers as superciliousness and personal animosity. Against these impressions teachers often build defenses. A small minority of drug-using or otherwise hostile students can transform a potential partner in the learning process into a resentful adversary. When a teacher loses enthusiasm and effectiveness, the learning of everybody in the class is diminished. This little-discussed dynamic is a central factor in the phenomenon called "teacher burnout" which has received so much attention in educational journals and conferences over the past ten years. This disaffection of teachers toward the very core of their work extends to other standard duties as well, especially conducting trips, chaperoning dances, monitoring assemblies—duties once thought to be a specially rewarding dimension of the job.

Although they are the most affected by the disaffection and hardening of their teachers, students often do not understand what causes those reactions. Non-using students see faculty defenses or desperate administrative measures restricting free movement through the school as repressive—and with some justice. Students complain that new restrictions and surveillance treat them "like little kids." These same students, however, rarely see the community and faculty concerns that bring about the administration's "repressive" measures. In this sure way, a minority of drug users can bring non-users into an uneasy, unpleasant relationship with school authorities. When this happens, school communities begin to behave as families do who have a drug-dependent member: as a house divided.

The way out is the promotion of a drug-free school. A school that wants to become and to remain drug free must strictly forbid drugs and drug use. When detected, drugs and their users should be removed from school. When a school can stand by this conviction, it should be broadcast—often and in the clearest terms—to all members of the community. This is done most effectively when a clear statement of no more than a page is drafted and sent to all families served by the school. The statement should be signed by the school board president of a public school; the chairman of the board of a private school; by the school's principal or headmaster; and by the head of its parent organization. Whatever the words, the statement should say:

> This school is committed to creating a drug-free climate for learning and growing up. Drug use and healthy child development are incompatible. Students who use, exchange, or are under the influence of alcohol or drugs in this school or any school-related event will be dismissed.

9.

PREVENTING STUDENT DRUG USE: EDUCATION AND INFORMATION

As long as illegal drugs are available to the extent that they are and students use them to the extent that they do, considerable time and energy will be, one way or another, given over by school staff to responding to the "drug problem." Working with using students and their families to try to halt students' drug use is in practice a time consuming and draining process. Working with recovering users to support their sobriety is similarly demanding. As a general rule, remediation of an existing drug problem is difficult and complex, and there is no guarantee that a given individual will respond to remedial measures; such is the allure and potency of intoxicating substances. By contrast, drug prevention measures require nothing "extra" in a school's program—although they may require change. Prevention measures should be aimed primarily at students before the age of initial exposure to alcohol and drugs in a peer setting. And, again in contrast to remediation, thoroughgoing prevention measures will have profound and lasting payoffs—provided they are augmented by the disciplinary policies, parent awareness measures, and other provisions discussed with respect to older students.

Drug prevention in a school should, so far as possible, take place within the existing instructional program. It should not consist exclusively of "special" presentations, nor should it be delegated to someone outside the regular instructional staff. At its best, a drug prevention program should commence in a highly rationalized, sequenced manner in kindergarten and proceed through the high school grades. The staff member responsible for coordinating curriculum should specify targeted concepts and factual information for each grade level, along with the staff members responsible for carrying it out (i.e., homeroom teacher, science teacher, health teacher, etc.). The very best drug education programs have been fashioned by school faculties themselves; these best suit a school's own structure and the teaching styles of its staff. Moreover, a faculty's developing its own drug education program is the surest way for it to educate itself about the actions of various drugs and their implications for child development.

Bearing in mind that there is no single "right" or "best" drug education curriculum, a suggested sequence of coverage might run as follows. In the early primary grades (Kindergarten through grade four, approximately ages five through nine), homeroom and/or science instruction might include a discrete teaching unit or periodic individual sessions on foods and medicines. The primary emphasis of this instruction should be nutrition and the maintenance of health. At the conceptual level, teachers and students should be introduced to the idea of body tissue and processes being fueled and maintained by what is taken into it. By the second grade and beyond, students should be able to understand the value of minimum daily requirements in the basic food groups: the importance of balance and moderation in diet. Built into these presentations and discussions should be a consideration of foods that taste specially good (sweets and other flavor-enhanced short order and "junk" food). Here students may learn that the intake of pleasing-tasting foods should be controlled to avoid dietary imbalance and health dangers ranging from tooth decay to heart disease later on. Learning to control what tastes/feels good in order to promote a greater good (productivity and health) is an eminently learnable lesson for primary schoolers. Taught convincingly and reinforced by home policies, these nutrition and pleasure-management lessons can do more to counter the "drug problem" later than any system of drug treatment.

Primary students ought also to learn the names and at least one basic property of the most common substances of abuse; nicotine, alcohol, and marijuana ought certainly to be discussed (others may be appropriate in different historical moments and in different regions). The distinctions between a medicine (a substance taken to alleviate pain or treat disease) and a drug (a substance taken for its pleasurable effects) should be taught, and it should be stressed and even belabored, that the same substance can in different circumstances be both medicine and drug. In the context of these discussions of specific substances and their effects, students should hear that drugs can produce such pleasing feelings that even strong and healthy people cannot resist them: it is very easy to get seriously sick—addicted—as a result of taking pleasure-producing chemicals. Even the earliest primary students should practice being on their guard against foods or other substances offered with the promise of making one "feel good." And again, the benefit of this instruction in school is greatly strengthened when school and families are in close enough communication to reinforce these lessons at home.

Lastly, primary students will greatly increase the likelihood of avoiding drug-related troubles ahead if their teachers and parents will work with them in ordinary decision-making. It is very possible for children to emerge at the brink of pubescence into circumstances where they are relatively mobile, comparatively free from supervision, and presented with dramatic choices for which their childhood experience has not prepared them. Children, even toddlers, should practice making decisions—this or that? Yes or no?—just as they practice anything else. For parents, this can be a tedious process, but it is nonetheless critical for healthy child development. If not always, at least often, pre-schoolers and primary students should be asked to decide on what to wear, not simply dressed. "The sandals or the sneakers?" "The red shirt or the white one?" are important exercises in early development. Choices about food are specially important (and especially tedious for parents!) "We have _____ things available for lunch—what would you like?" "What kind of sandwich?" "Milk or juice?" In this seemingly workaday way, children come to take control of their choices. Some decisions have consequences: "If we swim for another hour, there won't be time to cook dessert—what do you want to do?"

Intimately connected to a child's emergent decision-making ability are graduated exposures to unstructured time to be managed. If parents are affluent and farsighted enough, they can structure nearly all of a child's available after-school, weekend, and summer time with stimulating and improving activities. Children often accept these decisions on their behalf agreeably and appear even to thrive in the "program" of paid lessons, camps, and planned social outings. Serious—and to parents shocking—problems arise, however, when the seemingly productive and achieving child reveals an inability to resist rival "programs" when they present themselves: invitations to delinquency, drug and alcohol "parties."

Students are not likely to decline trouble—especially if urged by attractive and influential peers—unless they are practiced in declining. Over-programmed children often do not really "decide" to try a drug, they merely move on to whatever is happening next. A child's commonly expressed declaration, "I'm bored," ought not to be followed by "Well, let's find you something to do." Many children make their initial decision to use a drug because they don't know how to decline or because they can't see a reason to decline. Healthy primary school students should be encouraged, in controlled settings, to decide on outcomes and to make plans to achieve them. Moreover, pleasure should be a respected factor in decision-making, but not the dominant factor. Children passionately want—and should be encouraged—to control their circumstances, but this kind of self-mastery will never develop if either (1) there are no opportunities to practice it or (2) instant gratification is allowed to motivate a parent's or child's decision-making.

In the late primary or intermediate years (grades five and six), drug and alcohol use may be considered as a public health and social problem—as the "current event" it has in fact become. At this point the specific action of drugs, especially of cigarettes, alcohol, and marijuana, can be studied in more detail, including their effects on the brain, lungs, heart, and other internal organs. Here physicians, policemen, and other guest presenters may augment classroom instruction in a productive way. Outside speakers and films (discussion to follow) should be thoroughly previewed and, in the case of speakers, prepared before they are presented to students. Careful selection of these resources will prevent a contradictory or confused message. Teachers should be aware that physicians and law enforcement officers are not necessarily well informed on drug-related issues. Poor or misleading presentations from "experts" do more harm than no presentation. Outside resources should support and enhance the instruction given at school.

In the late primary years students are able to enter easily into simulation or "role-playing" experiences. It may on that account be profitable to discuss actual situations in which illegal drugs might first be offered and tried. After first thoroughly discussing with students what they should do if they observe/find/are offered a drug, various role-playing exercises can be set up in which students articulate and "practice" their responses. After each such simulation, those students observing it should be encouraged to evaluate and comment on what they have seen. A confident, practiced aversion to drugs on the part of fifth and sixth graders is a critical step in the creation of a drug-free school, as this age group is immediately adjacent to the middle schoolers for whom, as of this writing, a "first use" decision is likely to occur.

Middle schoolers (grades seven, eight, and sometimes nine) should be exposed to both prescriptive as well as descriptive drug education. As a student enters the middle school, he or she should be formally oriented to school rules, including those bearing on drugs. The rules forbidding drug use should be clearly connected to the health hazards of drug use already introduced in earlier grades and developed more fully in middle school health and science curricula. The period of rapid growth and development associated with adolescence, including emergent sexual maturity, should be discussed and charted for (and by) middle schoolers. This provides an excellent opportunity to discuss the effects of illegal drugs on these critical processes. Skillful teachers and counselors will be able to help early adolescents see why a period of rapid development and change can cause an intensified need for peer approval. When students see this, it is easy to point out why drug use, if an "in" group makes it a badge of peer approval, can be so attractive.

Middle school children invariably make idols of pop stars, athletic heroes, and attractive older students. Teachers must keep in mind that middle schoolers do not typically identify with "finished" adults, but rather with what they perceive to be the most effective representatives of the age group just ahead: mid- and late-teenagers. For this reason, in school systems in which the high school is drug-ridden, middle school efforts to be drug free are severely hampered.

For the same reason, middle school is a good time to have recovering users and effective non-users address the student body. Recovering users have experienced treatment and if they have an AA experience they can simply tell their story as honestly as they can. However well-intentioned, they should be screened in advance by middle school staff. The more "typical" the recovering student is in family background, school ability, and interests, the more instructive he will be to his middle school audience. One problem in relying on "hard cases," or reclaimed addicts, to tell the drug story is that non-users and early users perceive too great a gap between their experience and the speakers' to take them seriously. The right presentation from a recovering teenage user, however, can be an unforgettable deterrent to drug use. So, in addition, can a perceptive presentation from older non-users. These students do best when they realistically chart the drug and party "scene" at the high school level and share their own motivations and techniques for staying drug free, along with their perceived benefits in doing so.

In the high school grades drug education should be a standard and substantial component of required health courses. It should also be a topic of special inquiry and discussion in biology classes (required in most schools), especially when the nervous system, endocrine system, and other drug-affected systems and body sites are studied. Curricular instruction may also be helpfully supplemented by outside speakers, preferably with a sound scientific background. A good use of an outside speaker, particularly one known to be effective, is for him to address in assembly the entire student body, then perhaps meet with selected classes, be available for a few unstructured "open" forums, and meet with the Core Group and faculty at day's end to share impressions. The Core Group, perhaps in concert with the science faculty, should also select current, scientifically sound, and reasonably accessible articles and books to be on reserve in a clearly designated part of the school's library. The experience of many schools that have done so is that students who would under no circumstances share a drug concern with a Core Group member or with any other teacher will read exhaustively through drug literature made available at school.

The capacity for sophistication reached by many high school students creates excellent opportunities for drug education, although the very best of it may be successfully "defended against" by users. Drug information sessions in the high school, in whatever classroom or format, should begin by acknowledging that drugs, like sex, are an uncomfortable thing to talk about in a school setting because of the kinds of feelings around and because they are associated with serious disciplinary policies. Once the limitations are acknowledged, an atmosphere may be established in which fresh inquiry may take place. Students typically interact with friends and adults who have pronounced attitudes, pro and con, about drug use, but they rarely hear from anybody, including physicians, teachers, and parents, who demonstrate a convincing mastery of current biochemical and medical facts. Teachers who so inform themselves will not only change what students think, they will change the way they think.

A promising structure for high school drug education—one that has been demonstrated to be effective at several schools—is first to run students through a thoroughgoing short course on the developmental psychology of adolescence, then to introduce the actions of various drugs, inviting students to hypothesize (and recognize) the effects of those actions on development. Teachers might prepare themselves by reading (or reviewing) the model of adolescent psycho-sexual development proposed by Erik Erikson in *Childhood and Society* and *Identity, Youth, and Crisis* (Norton). Interesting and useful background is also included in Kagan and Coles' excellent anthology, *12 to 16: Early Adolescence* (also Norton). The theory of adolescent cognitive development put forward by the Swiss developmental psychologist, Jean Piaget, is also fascinating to review, particularly in light of the losses to it that follow from drug use. Whereas middle schoolers are often impervious to instruction and introspection about psychological development, older adolescents have enough perspective on their own—and the cognitive capacity—to become thoroughly engaged in it.

Once a class is fairly well grounded in the biological changes that commence in adolescence and has further considered the "normal" defenses and adaptations to those changes (including moodiness, bouts of hypersensitivity, intensified reliance on peer approval, drives to separate oneself from authority and to feel autonomous, especially in how one manages time), it is time to introduce a consideration of the various illegal drugs. Once the known actions of the depressants, stimulants, and hallucinogens are presented, students are ready to be challenged with the critical issue: how do drugs alter healthy development?

"Stress management" might well emerge as one organizing concept in the discussion that follows. The background in the biological and psychological changes will underscore for students the point that stress is not only "normal" during these years, it is necessary for maturation and learning. Effective classroom teaching and effective coaching might fairly be considered a process by which students and players are introduced to heightened (but manageable) levels of stress which they strive to alleviate by changing behavior: by learning. Learning a new operation in mathematics, or how to document research, or how to "trap" an opposing lineman, or how to "get" a character one has been cast to play—each is stimulated in part by the stress of having to do so. The assignment creates the stress; mastering it alleviates it—with a residue of new skill, pride in accomplishment, enhanced status, and so on. Students who see the dynamics of this process should be asked what other measures, besides mastery, might alleviate stress (answer: cheating, quitting, not trying, putting down the effort at hand as "stupid," the province of "dumb jocks" or "eggheads" or "nerds"). Students will supply endless examples. These "other defenses" may well alleviate stress, and they may even occasion a kind of illusory "respect," but they cannot deliver mastery. And nothing, of course, blocks stress management and preempts mastery as devastatingly as drug use does. Drugs which both interfere with function and reward the loss with profoundly pleasurable sensations do more than block stress management; they replace it. Students who undergo stress—who even subject themselves to extra amounts of it—to ace a test or to write an honors thesis or to run faster do so for the non-sensual pleasure of mastery. If earlier child development has placed sensual gratification over mastery, and if the means to it are available, drug-induced pleasure will replace mastery every time. For such individuals, appeals to what they are losing or what they are missing are not convincing; they are already—without much effort, without skill, and (at first) without stress—hitting the pleasure jackpot. Non-users avoid drugs because of the stress they imagine they would feel if drugs interfered with their performance or compromised their standards. They have an especially hard time understanding drug users who have never learned to manage stress at all. A fine British film of the eighties, *Chariots of Fire*[8], a true story about British athletes of the twenties, is remarkably effective in illustrating the relationship between pleasure, stress and mastery.

Once again a teacher should experience little difficulty in pointing out and having students share the stresses inherent to adolescence. The special stresses connected to early dating alone can lend to productive (and hilarious) discussion. But when the

---

[8]*Chariots of Fire* can be purchased for school use or rented in VHS or Beta Max video tape for a modest sum. Films in general should be used with great caution in drug education. Those made specifically for schools are rarely effective. Drug jargon, paraphernalia and student dress styles date quickly; such that intentionally "with it" educational films are easy to laugh at by student audiences. Films that show a good deal of actual drug use and which are also accompanied by contemporary rock music scores can be downright stimulating to student viewers. A reliable guideline is to preview with students all drug-related films—and to use them sparingly. The complexity of the phenomenon is generally not expressed in film or television treatments.

stress of such a necessary phase of social and sexual development is modified from the outset by alcohol and drug use, elementary kinds of maturation may never occur at all. The data of child development and drug pharmacology and logic will confirm this for the instructor; the data observable at weekend "parties" will confirm it for the student who takes care to look.

10.

STARTING A PARENT AWARENESS NETWORK

Less than a percent of the nation's school children attend boarding schools; the rest live at home. Consequently the typical school's program of drug awareness and drug education cannot of itself insure a drug-free climate for youth. Parents have got to help, and in order to do so, they have to inform and organize themselves. Here once again the PRIDE organization in Atlanta can offer assistance in the form of sharing effective parent network models that have proved serviceable in communities throughout the country and also by putting inquirers in direct touch with seasoned parent groups. As with school programs, the point is to get started. The "energizer," or agent of change, may be an informed, concerned parent—often one who has been through a family ordeal with a drug using child—or a persuasive member of the school staff or an inspiring outsider. Some parent awareness groups operate as a permanent subcommittee of a PTA or general parents' organization; others are unaffiliated and value that autonomy. Either approach can work.

Once the concern and interest level of some parents, even a small minority, is aroused, the larger parent body should be invited to an open meeting to share community-wide responses to student drug use. A stimulating speaker may provide a "keynote" address but the agenda of the meeting should be the identification of the problem of drink and drug use by school-aged children and the initiation of response to it. The tone of early meetings is critical to the success of later ones. Many parents, particularly those who have had drug problems in their families or have otherwise observed them first hand, are frightened and angry about the drug phenomenon. Fear and anger, however, may impede the organization and coordination of a parents' movement. Although there is much in the contemporary drug scene to be fearful and angry about, appeals made on the basis of such feelings turn many families away from further involvement. If the anti-drug concerns are too stridently expressed, they may be dismissed as a bee up the bonnet of "fanatics" or "witch hunters." Parents put off or made to feel defensive by the tone of anti-drug spokesmen may counter by denying the seriousness of the drug problem and subsequently ignoring it.

The fact of the matter is that most parents, whether "permissive" or strict, whether active in civic activities or not are interested in the drug problem, potential or actual. Moreover, parents are likely to become increasingly interested as they learn more about the actions of drugs and about the process of child development. For this reason, early parent forums might well be informational, perhaps drawing on the same educational resources used in the high school drug education program. Before organizing formally, parents should be informed of the effects of the most common drugs available to children, should have at least an approximate estimate of the extent of drug use in the community served by the school, and should share a conviction that the use of mood-altering chemicals poses a serious threat to the education and maturation of their children. If the school has already begun to address the drug problem, and if, in consequence, new disciplinary policies, a Core Group, support groups, etc., have been established, parents should be informed (or reminded) of all these developments and of the commitments that have brought them into being. Knowing "where the school stands" and why can be a valuable boost in motivating parents.

A parent group to promote drug-free youth (in some communities called Parent Networks or Parent Awareness Groups) actually comes into existence with a common action: a pledge to support a common anti-drug policy. The exact form and wording—even the substance—of these pledges vary from community to community, but a typical one might read as follows:

As parents served by the _____ school system, we support the concept of a Parent Awareness Network and would like to become part of it. As network members I/we
  1. Agree not to serve alcohol or other illegal substances to children below legal age, nor to

allow these substances to be consumed by minors at our house.
2. Agree to supervise gatherings of youngsters at our house, to determine in advance the size of such gatherings and the time they will take place.
3. Wish to be informed, without judgment, by other Network parents of any drinking or drug use they have observed on the part of my children.
4. Agree to inform, without judgments, other Network parents of drink· or drug use I/we have observed on the part of their children.

Signed _____
Address _____
Phone _____

The pledges returned comprise the initial Network directory which can be distributed to all families served by the school, with an invitation to sign on if families for some reason forgot to respond or missed earlier information. It is a good idea to send early Network mailings to the entire parent body, even to those who at first express opposition to it. For one thing, the whole community being apprised of the anti-drug activities of active parents and by the school dispels false information and, to an extent, supports even non-Network families in their resolve to curb drug use. Clear and comprehensive communications also win new members.

It is often difficult to tell what a community's initial response to a Parent Network will be. In some communities, virtually the whole parent body signs on at once. In others, despite well-planned programs and appeals, the initial response is cautious. Whatever the case, any membership at all can be a promising start. Without exception, the terms of Network membership, however straightforward (see PLEDGE), will raise numerous parent questions and requests for clarification. Clarification sessions should be called as soon as possible after the directory is completed.

Typically, Network provisions about not serving intoxicants to minors and agreeing to supervise parties are comparatively easy to agree upon. Questions do arise, however, as to whether the prohibition of alcohol should extend to serving it to one's own children on festive occasions in family settings. This is a thorny question, except for those families whose religious practice forbids alcohol entirely. For those who accept social drinking for adults—and the vast majority of western peoples do—the use of alcohol in a controlled family setting is the only acceptable orientation to alcohol use available in a society. Moreover, even concerned parents enthusiastically disposed to networking may balk at what they perceive to be interference with their own family decision-making at its most responsible. Nevertheless, serving alcohol to children at home does convey "mixed messages," and the more concrete the thinking of a child the more mixed the message—despite parent protests to the contrary. The most workable solution is for Network agreements *not* to infringe on family practices which are not in violation of the law (which in most jurisdictions means that parents might legally offer their children a glass of wine at a holiday meal). Parents who simply do not serve any alcohol to children underage under any circumstances will have the easiest time justifying their other concerns and policies about drink and drugs. It is worth examining seriously the claim sometimes put forward by parents that "I don't mind my teenage son or daughter having a social beer from time to time, because I don't want him to be naive when he comes in contact with the actual drinking that goes on over the weekends. After all, he or she is going to see enough of it in college. We've got to be 'realistic.' " However plausible-sounding on first hearing, this claim cannot be supported by the actual drinking practices of minors. There is no indication whatsoever that children "learn" social drinking in illicit drinking bouts and at unchaperoned "parties." More typically, they get drunk, many intentionally, others unintentionally. Nor is social drinking difficult to learn. For those who maintain that it is, the wisest policy would be to delay the course until the novice has as much critical intelligence and maturity as possible—at *least* until the age of legal consent. The fact of the matter is that the consumption of alcoholic beverages by children in any setting achieves no important good, and it can open the door to a substantial, enduring harm. A child is deprived of nothing important if he is not given alcohol at home. Historical climates differ. In the current one, the clearer the antidrink and drug signal the better.

Even thornier problems arise over the provisions in the Network agreement committing parents "to inform, without judgment" other parents of known drinking and drug-taking incidents on the part of their children. In practice, this is easier to promise than to do. The resistance to informing other parents of their children's drunkenness or drug dealing is easily understandable. Not only is very worrying news being conveyed, the information exchange also raises feelings ranging from shame, to defensiveness, to defenselessness on the part of the party receiving the news, while the party bearing it feels guilty for doing so. When the families do not know each other, the bad feelings can be intensified. To these difficulties are added another serious one. Much of what parents know about the social scene through which their children move comes from them, in casual conversation, in the car, over the breakfast table. There is a real and substantial danger that when information dropped or volunteered at home finds its way into other households, the open communication between parent and child may close up. Children are often adamant that their parents not "narc" (inform) on the delinquencies of their friends and classmates. They do this because, quite understandably, they don't want to see friends in trouble, they also don't want to face the hostility, possible rejection, and, in extreme cases, the physical reprisals they will get if they are linked with someone's being "busted."

In practice, Network agreement or not, most parents are willing to risk relaying drug-related news if they are convinced that there is danger to a child's health or even his life. In less dramatic circumstances there is a reluctance to get involved. Unfortunately the dramatic cases will continue to crop up, unless parents can overcome their reluctance. This must become the central thrust of an effective parents' organization. There are a number of ways to overcome this very natural resistance. The first is proposing the Network agreement itself; in signing up, a parent must say, perhaps for the first time, "This is a real problem, and I am obligated to *do* something about it." Network leaders and facilitators (discussion of them to follow) should ask parents in their general meetings if they really do want to hear about their children's drinking and drug use away from home. The answer is always a resounding yes. This is the moment to point out that there will be no such information unless the other side of the bargain—a willingness to communicate incidents—is kept. Network members must work to convince the tentative and the skeptical that letting children's experiments with intoxication progress into chemical dependency is the worst outcome possible. Preventing it is worth a moment's apprehension before dialing, a little embarrassment, even getting some (undeserved) flack from defensive parents—"and just where did you get *that* information?" Even when other parents don't take bad news graciously, they take it in. And this may be the beginning of corrective action. The writer has recently heard from a Network parent who said, "Well, I did what I was told. When I saw _____ staggering drunk getting out of a car after _____, I phoned his parents and told them as plainly and as nicely as I could what I saw—and I took *hell* for it. I was cross-examined for half an hour, and none too pleasantly. That's the last time I do that!" She was of course urged to "hang in there," especially since, as it happens, the irate parents have confronted their son's drinking, energetically and effectively, for the first time.

Several parent groups have found a way around the problematic commitment to inform other parents of their children's drink and drug-related troubles. In place of direct calls to other parents, they instead register (or have the option to register) the concern to the school's faculty Core Group (see previous discussion of Core Group, p. 16). Parents may either call a school number and file the concern or they can fill out a short "concern slip" in the school's administrative office. Network parents are made aware that concerns registered with the Core Group do not initiate disciplinary reprisals of any kind. Nor do they necessarily occasion even a Core Group interview with the student named. The Core Group, for its part, monitors the concern slips along with school-registered concerns about possible drug use. When a confirmed pattern emerges, the Core Group confronts the student and, as already discussed, contacts his family. There are real strengths and a few weaknesses to this system of networking. On the positive side, the school's Core Group has more and better data to work from; the "in-school" and "out-of-school" faces of a student's drug problem begin to corroborate each other and to make sense. Because "concern slips" may be filed anonymously, there is less reluctance to register them. But while all of this relieves some Network members of the anxiety connected with direct, family-family communications, it also raises anxiety from other members. The idea that some adult knows about one's child's intoxication, but that the information may never come back to the parent of the child affected can be very disagreeable. Other parents are uncomfortable with the anonymity of "concern slips"; for them the prospect of an anonymous "file" building up somewhere in the school makes them nervous. The discomfort tends to be eased as Network members come to know each other better and to trust each other.

Generally speaking, the readiness of Network members to cooperate with one another and to keep the agreement is a result of the clarity of network communication and of the effectiveness of its leadership. Apart from a convinced commitment to drug-free youth, a Network leader should primarily be a coordinator and a facilitator. Since the very nature of networking is a partnership among equals, there is not much need for hierarchical organization. An ad hoc, self-appointed committee typically sets a network in motion, after which officers can be selected from volunteers out of the full membership. A subcommittee might be established to compile, distribute, and update the directory. Another might be responsible for disseminating current scientific, legal, and educational information bearing on drug use to the Network membership. Another might organize special forums and arrange for speakers and other special presentations. Still another might coordinate activities with Networks from adjacent schools and communities. Once a general membership has been established, a sub-network should be established by school grade level (i.e., a seventh grade network, eighth grade network, etc.) with a parent chairman for each class. Once in motion, Network business typically takes place in small committee meetings, class network meetings, or sub-networks within a class.

The important job of coordinating committee work, the class networks, and the network-school relationship must be assumed by a skillful and energetic Network chairman. The man or woman who takes this on must have sufficient time to devote to it, for a Network organization becomes easily amorphous and uncoordinated if its various sub-activities and projects lack direction and focus. Volunteer organizations, especially those generated by a single issue, are inclined to invest their initial energy into the first scheme proposed to it; if this initial scheme doesn't happen to contribute to the goal of drug-free youth, then, in the long run, the time and effort are resented by the membership. One common temptation for beginning parent groups is the urge to repeat the experience that first inspired the person or people who organized the Network. When this happens, the business of the parent group becomes exclusively organizing and then attending special programs and speeches by "experts." Programs and speakers may be stimulating and useful resources for the fledgling parent organization—and they create a reassuring collective sense of "something being done"—but they do not of themselves correct the problem of youthful drinking and drug-taking. It is relatively easy for a parents' organization to become "about" itself. The real job—changing the climate in which youth make decisions—takes place between parents and children as they hammer out home policies and consequences, as drug-free social experiences are planned and executed as alternatives to the current "party" or "concert" scene, as parents, teachers, and children begin to share information and to confront drug users and their families. These things are the proper business of a Parent Network, and the Network chairman's chief task is to maintain these things as central.

The Network chairman must also take pains not to avoid "factions," which is impossible, but to accommodate them as gracefully as possible in service of Network goals. Once again, anti-drug sentiment has an inherent appeal to self-styled "conservatives" who see drug use as an inevitable plague resulting from the policies of those more "liberal." Network founders are often of such a mind. "Liberals," for their part, often respond negatively to the perceived puritanism of anti-drug efforts and want to resist impeding the developing freedom, with all its risks, of their teenagers; they don't want to violate their children's "trust" with excessive surveillance. In the disparity between these two viewpoints lies potential war. Skillful diplomacy on the part of Network leaders, however, can make use of the good energies of both groups. There is ample target for the righteous indignation of the "conservatives": for instance, the presence in nearly any commercial district of any size of "head shops" or other outlets for drug-using paraphernalia, commerce which has no conceivably redeeming benefit, and which is targeted directly at children. The "liberals" who want to see their children free to take risks and learn from them can be made allies in the anti-drug cause when they are helped to see that pleasure-producing drugs are the surest thieves of freedom and choice. The independence and productivity and health all parents want for their children is imperilled to the extent that early drug use becomes a factor in maturation. At the risk of belaboring the point, Network parents need not share any conventionally "political" positions at all: only a commitment to a drug-free youth.

Networking owes its name to the concept of activity extending inwards and outwards in service of a common mission. Once a network of parents from a single school or a school district is formed, and its purposes and goals are defined, it will want to extend itself inward and outward. Class networks—that is, parents' groups organized by school grade—have already been mentioned. These groups and even smaller sub-networks consisting of the parents of various friendship groups are perhaps in a position to be most effective. They are able to meet in more comfortable surroundings in someone's yard or living room—and are in the best position to know what the range of social activity actually is at a given grade level. It is in these smaller, informal sub-network groups that parents are often greatly relieved to realize that the battles they have been fighting, they believed alone, against the jaded and libertine standards of what they understood, from their children's reports, to be "other people's parents" are almost universally shared. Through talking and listening to other parents, common expectations and policies will emerge fluidly and naturally. Occasions for parents to discuss "parenting," rare enough otherwise, ought to be the central business of a Network.

There are also benefits of extending a Network outward: to adjacent networks, to merchandisers, to law enforcement agencies, to political jurisdictions, to the press, to libraries, and, as discussed already, to the schools. At present, many record stores, small, convenient-hours food stores, boutiques, and "head shops" display a variety of drug-related products, including items like a commercial deodorant can to conceal drug "stashes"; aids to smoking or inhaling drugs ("roach clips" for grasping unholdable ends of marijuana cigarettes, various kinds of pipes); non-psychoactive or non-regulated substances used to enhance or adulterate illegal drugs; incenses to cover drug odors; cocaine spoons and inhalers; rolling papers for marijuana; "practice" or mini-highs such as N^2O cartridges, and the apparatus to inhale the gas; and an ever expanding array of other paraphernalia. Parents often have to enter these stores and have the products pointed out to them to believe that such things are available commercially; children do not. Some cities and towns have succeeded in driving out "head shops" through local legislation; other attempts are still being battled in the courts.[9] But even if high courts allow the sale of drug paraphernalia on the grounds that to do otherwise is an infringement on the seller's and the consumer's civil liberties, there are other effective means of driving them away or changing the line of products. If Parent Network representatives, working with or through local chambers of commerce, confront store owners with their firm but courteous disapproval of drug-related products, this alone can bring about the removal of the offending products—

[9]In a headshop visited by the writer, the proprietor countered a complaint registered about a bong (elaborate water-cooled marijuana pipe) for sale by saying, "a lot of people like to plant flowers in them."

provided they were a peripheral, not the central, line of merchandise. Out-and-out "head shops" which resist community criticism can be written up extensively through local news coverage and through an indefatigable stream of letters-to-editors. Both irony and outrage are acceptable responses—and both are legal. And of course the surest way to dry up the drug-paraphernalia industry is to dry up the market for it through the creation of a drug-free youth.

Parent Networkers have also been successful in helping to frame and pass local government ordinances requiring that youth gatherings—parties—be supervised by attendant adults and that no illegal beverages or other substances be served; stiff fines (often a required minimum of a thousand dollars) are imposed on the parents of the host in the event of a violation. Where enforced, these ordinances have been very effective, an excellent example of community action supporting school and family concerns. The ordinances, however, mean little unless there is a commitment on behalf of the police to enforce them. This commitment does not always follow in the wake of the ordinances. Breaking up and assigning responsibility for a large, rackety teenage party is a messy and unpleasant business; local police, who are sometimes neighbors and friends of the families involved, often back away from the task. But they should not, and vigilant, concerned parents should not let them. Acting in the face of unpleasantness is simply the price concerned members of a community may have occasionally to pay in order to regain control of the environment in which older children make decisions.

Finally, it is important for Networking parents to be formally in touch with other Networks from nearby schools, adjacent school districts, and neighboring communities. Communicating, interlocking Networks can share directories, share programs, share medical resources, and most importantly share experiences. The society is generally mobile, and children from driving age onward are mobile. The friends they make and activities they attend are usually not limited to those in their own school or even in their own community. In typical residential communities, public school, parochial school, and independent school students intermingle freely. In suburban areas it is not uncommon for a teenager's social orbit to span four or five abutting communities on a fifteen mile radius from his or her house. In such a social configuration a single school or a single school's parent body cannot be entirely effective in altering the climate of drug use—although a single community can start.

Network affiliation may require a few evenings' time each year and, depending on a parent's interest, some other commitments as well. By no means, however, should anything in the foregoing suggest that Network activity is likely to dominate a family's home life. *Most* of a Network's obligation lies in agreeing to its basic terms and trying to keep them. The real business of Parent Networking is not meetings, forums, and committee work. The real business is the understanding forged over the dining table or in the living room between parents and their children about how each family is going to shape and respond to decisions about the use of alcohol and other drugs. Very simply, every family should have an explicit policy, with clearly stated (and kept) consequences for violations. In this intra-family process lies much of the success or failure of Parent Networking.

ACTION AND VALUES: FOOD FOR THOUGHT

Mobilizing a school to confront and reverse the youthful drug epidemic is not an objective, "value-free" enterprise. Nor is it, like environmental responsibility, *merely* a scientifically sensible undertaking—although it could not be more scientifically sensible. As with most seemingly obvious social issues, if two or three "why" questions are posed seriously, defenders of the "issue" are thrown back on their most deeply held personal values. For instance, why oppose current patterns of drug use? Because young people are being diminished and even lost. Why be concerned about this? Because they are part of, or will become part of, the social fabric which sustains civilized living, including my own life. Why be concerned about this? Because—because why? Because, damn it, you simply know in your bones it is right. Because you know some of these people and love them. Because, as religious people might say, that's not the way God intended life to be. Such things are rarely stated in committee meetings or in editorials. In fact, such things are rarely acknowledged to oneself. Yet these are the real reasons, the real motivators. These are values.

Values and value questions, as critical and unavoidable as they are, tend to make twentieth century people uncomfortable. We are so diverse and so pluralistic and so well-schooled about the evils of intolerance that it is easy to adopt a vague social philosophy of "you do your thing, and I'll do mine" without qualification. Even extensively educated people can be heard saying, "Do whatever you like, but don't impose your values on me" (or on my children at school, etc.). This view stems, whether intentionally or not, from a philosophy of ethical relativism. According to ethical relativism, value statements contain no meaning in themselves. That is, a person who says, "*Gandhi* is a better movie than *Deep Throat*" is conveying nothing true or meaningful about *Gandhi* or *Deep Throat,* although he is conveying something true about himself: his orientation to those films and anything that orientation might, given further analysis, imply. Values, according to this outlook, are relative to those who hold them and cannot be arbitrated by a common, true standard. But while a logically consistent point of view, ethical relativism causes serious problems (because of its very inability to resolve serious problems). Since ethical relativists have no grounds except personal "psychological" ones for preferring one value over another, some "relativistic" arbiter must decide between competing value claims. The aribiter preferred might be majority rule. Or it might be violent force. But which? There is the problem. Ethical relativism cannot commend one over the other. The majority of people may prefer majority rule, but what would commend that preference to the minority? Some sense of fairness or of due process? Such things do not objectively exist, according to ethical relativism.

    The fact of the matter is that compelling, binding value commitments make no sense if ethical relativism is true, yet many contemporary citizens seem to want to have it both ways: to hold true, important values but not to acknowledge the values claims of others. Such people are quite likely to say in the course of a conversation, "Now you are making a value judgment," as if that implied a logical mistake. But holding values, arguing and acting in reference to them is not a logical mistake, nor necessarily any other kind of mistake. The mistake may be ethical relativism, however widely it is distributed.

    For most of civilized history, ethical relativism has not been a dominant or very compelling doctrine. It came up but was forcefully countered in several of the dialogues of Plato (Fourth Century B.C.). The position also takes rather a beating in both Old and New Testament scripture. Pontius Pilate, for example, the Roman official in Jerusalem responsible for approving Jesus' execution, responds to Jesus's statement that his role is to bear witness to the truth, by asking, "What is truth?" This is straightforward ethical relativism. The primary mission of *Biblical* prophets from Nathan through Isaiah can be seen as an attempt to align men's practical affairs with what is universally true.

The opposite of ethical relativism is ethical idealism: the view that values may be grounded in something objectively true, because objective truth (whether divinely or naturally given) exists. Objective truth is what judgments and all other kinds of thinking should aim at, because everything else, logically, will be a mistake. Both classical philosophy and all western religious thought are "idealistic" in that they acknowledge the existence of objective, eternal truth. For idealists, value questions ("should I keep commitments?") are the same family as fact questions ("Is Cleveland in Ohio?"), only much harder. But however hard, value questions are finally unavoidable. They are certainly unavoidable in facing a serious social problem like drug abuse. For most individuals who take on the problem, it will help to be a little introspective, to identify the values motivating one's actions. It is hard to stand by one's values unless one has really paused to consider what they are. If they can't be reached, can't be named, it will be very hard to maintain one's momentum when challenged with the accusations and hard feelings drug prevention activity usually elicits. For sometimes, the motivating values, if examined honestly, are not very substantial. The school administrator may, at the nub, want nothing more than for the school to *look good* so that he in turn will look good in the eyes of his constituents and his superiors. A parent may agree to join an awareness Network because he or she would not want to be thought irresponsible by others in the community. Such values, which are real enough, are not likely to carry one far into drug prevention. For at heart these values and many others, are self-regarding, not youth- or society-regarding. It is possible for clever people to realize these values—to look good, to be thought responsible—without effectively addressing the drug problem at all.

The values question is very personal—but also unavoidable in drug abuse prevention. In the introductory section of this book a case was made that drug use itself, not a clear shift in political attitudes, was the primary cause of the drug problem. This thesis is stressed in the hope that no more futile effort be extended a variety of false "underlying" causes; for it has now been well established that whatever personal or social problems may underly it, drug use is the problem as long as it is engaged in. The neurosis afflicting a neurotic drug user cannot be put right until the drug use stops. For many chemically dependent people, there are not classifiable personality problems other than drug use, and when it is terminated, life resumes productively. But this is not to say there is *no* connection between prevailing social attitudes and drug use, for there is no question that when there is a clear social consensus which forbids or strictly limits alcohol and drug use, patterns of experimentation and abuse are affected.

This point was made especially clear when considering the experience of some of the school communities examined in preparation for this book. Two religious schools in particular, one a "fundamentalist" Christian school, the other an orthodox Jewish school, provide instructive examples. In addition to their strong religious affiliations, these schools differ from typical American middle schools and high schools in a number of other important respects. Both are "intimate" school communities, small enough so that it is easy for students and teachers to know every other member of the school by name and for the families of the students to be acquainted with each other. Both schools also see no distinction in emphasis between academic program and character development. The religious values on which the schools are founded shape the curriculum and the behavioral expectations of the students. The educational philosophies of both schools see education as being in the service of profound, all-encompassing religious values. Take away the values—the aim—and there is no purpose or direction to education. Education for itself, whatever the intellectual facility achieved, could be a danger, could be put in service of an inhumane or otherwise harmful goal. Both schools define themselves as part of a three-way partnership among church/temple, school, and family, each part sharing fundamental values. Neither school, incidentally, has a drug program—beyond a rule stating that drinking and drug use are forbidden. No more is considered necessary because the families affiliated with these schools also share a consensus that intoxication is inherently wrong, disgraceful and inherently at odds with divinely mandated love and service. In neither of these schools is there a "drug problem."

Do these schools have something to teach the American educational establishment? They may—and the lesson is not necessarily the massive conversion of American schools into small, intensely religious ones. The message may, however, be a hard one to hear:

that unless communities in which children are nurtured can build a consensus out of shared values and can act accordingly, the "drug problem" will not only persist, it will flourish. The drug problem will flourish because the drug culture has a value system, too. It is a value system which says, "The supreme value is pleasurable sensations, damn the price." In the absence of anything stronger and clearer, this value will stand. Those seeking to understand the "drug problem" could do worse than to examine societies and organizations that don't have it.

SUMMARY

Responding effectively to student drug use begins and ends with values. Without an unshakable conviction that developing the physical, intellectual, artistic, and spiritual promise of children is an aim superior to—and incompatible with—the pursuit of chemically induced pleasure, there is no solution to the problem.

Once that conviction is held by an individual or group within a school, then a multi-step program may be articulated and executed. The first step is acknowledging the nature and extent of the problem on the part of the school's policy-makers, including the school principal or headmaster. The acknowledgement should be shared openly with all the school's constituents: students, parents, school board, and the community-at-large. The acknowledgement should be paired from the outset to a stated commitment to making the school drug free and a straightforward appeal for help in doing so. Those first convinced of the problem must arm themselves sufficiently with local and national data to overcome the two principal obstacles to an effective response to drug use: ignorance and denial of a problem "in our community."

Once the conviction is held and a problem acknowledged, those most concerned can begin a program of action. The first step in a heretofore unmobilized school is to present good information to all constituents. Through such organizations as The American Council on Drug Education in Rockville, Maryland, PRIDE in Atlanta, or through the National Institute on Drug Abuse (NIDA) in Rockville, Maryland, current, readable printed matter can be acquired inexpensively. A few well-promoted parent forums or conferences on drug abuse issues featuring speakers of known quality may also serve well as a "kick-off" event for more systematic measures to follow.

Once the level of awareness has been raised in the school community, the next step is to orient the whole teaching faculty, including coaches and support staff, to the phenomenon of youthful drug use. This may be done through in-service training days, a series of such days, or through whatever process a school normally uses for all-faculty meetings. The presenter at these sessions may be an outside speaker or someone within the school structure or parent body who has been thoroughly versed in the social phenomenon of youthful drug use, its educational and medical consequences, and the most workable responses to it. It does not matter whether this presenter is a physician, an educator, a teacher or a parent. The goal, again, of this initial faculty orientation is to create or to strengthen the school's consensus that drug use of any kind is unacceptable for developing children, and to offer ways to stop it.

From the most interested and committed faculty a Core Group should be formed who will receive intensive training in recognizing, confronting, and responding to drug use. Once trained, the Core Group can act as (1) a repository for drug-related observations and information from faculty, parents, and students, (2) a purveyor of further drug education for faculty and students, (3) counselors who confront directly students whose behavior suggests a possibility of drug use or who are known to be involved with drugs, and (4) resources for parents concerned about their children's drug involvement or who may need referral to treatment or other services outside the school. It should be the Core Group's responsibility to educate the school community about the stages by which a casual user of drugs can become a dependent user.

At every step taken by the school to confront a student's possible drug involvement, the student's parents should be contacted. The key to curbing drug abuse, whether by prevention or remediation, is to form a school-family partnership based on shared convictions and complementary policies. When parents begin to see the school staff as allies in their efforts to raise their children drug free, they will begin to volunteer observations and concerns of their own which might stop an incipient drug problem from becoming a full blown one. To be effective in this partnership, school staff, especially the Core Group, must train itself to hear, to bear, and to support others when they receive bad news.

When a student's drug use, discovered through disciplinary action or through Core Group activity, is found to be chronic or possibly chronic, he or she should be referred for treatment, beginning with a formal evaluation. Core Group members should investigate treatment programs in advance so that they can be helpful to parents when a student is in trouble with drugs. If school policy permits, and if the student in treatment and his or her family wishes to reenter the school after treatment, then the Core Group should facilitate reentry, accommodating post-treatment needs of the user to the realities of school schedules and requirements.

Core Group members may also find it worthwhile to facilitate a student support group for recovering users and for any other students who would like to have help staying drug free. Support groups work best when they are facilitated by someone (at best a Core Group member) trained to do so. Sessions should be regularly scheduled before, during, or after the school day and should consist primarily of non-directed exchanges from students of the experiences at home and in school as they work at staying drug free. Support groups should maintain confidentiality about what is discussed in regular sessions, but they should make their existence and purpose known to the whole school community—even to the extent of making special presentations to the student and parent bodies.

Offering diagnostic and remedial services will not of themselves diminish the incidence of drug use in a school. The climate of consequences in which students make drug-related decisions must be altered by the establishment and enforcement of firm rules and discipline. Health consequences, learning consequences, and social consequences of drug use often seem too remote to inhibit a student from experimenting with a drug. School discipline is immediate, and when the rule itself and disciplinary procedures relating to it are carried through forcefully, students will make different decisions about using and exchanging drugs at school. The recommended school drug policy—the one demonstrated to have the most deterrent effect—is one that states that students who use, exchange, or who are under the influence of drugs at school or at a school-related event should be dismissed. In public school systems where state statutes make dismissal impossible, violators should at least be removed from school until the school has been given an acceptable assurance that the student is drug free and will continue to be drug free. A school change (including movements both ways between public and private schools) should not be considered a necessarily injurious consequence of student drug use. The faculty Core Group should stand ready to assist families in arranging school changes or mandatory home-study periods for students caught violating school drug policies.

The school that adopts a strict "no second chance" drug policy must be prepared to weather some parental and student storms—although these typically occur at the outset of the new policy and can be assuaged greatly if the reasons for the policy are communicated clearly to all school constituents. Very shortly after implementation of the new policy, drug-related incidents usually begin to decrease dramatically. Many schools, especially private schools which have more latitude in dismissals, have found that there are fewer dismissals with a strict policy than with a lenient one. A school which does not decisively separate drug use from the educational process in any way it can helps to accommodate youthful drug use.

In addition to the detection, confrontation, and disciplinary action measures discussed above, the school must design a continuing, highly rationalized sequence of drug education experiences punctuating the school curriculum from the primary grades through high school. Drug prevention curriculum should be developed—at best, by the school's own teaching staff—for kindergarten through grade six. Students should be oriented against illicit chemical pleasures before they reach an age (currently between twelve and sixteen in the United States) when a social opportunity to try a drug is likely. Aside from information about drugs' names and some of their documented effects on health, emphasis in the "pre-exposure" years should be placed on decision-making about forbidden substances. Role playing and other exercises in which children actually practice declining illegal substances are promising drug prevention measures.

In middle schools and beyond, drug education—both curricular and special programs—should be a structured component of a school's overall program, but they will not by themselves turn around students already involved with drugs. So while middle schools and high schools are emphatically the right starting places for new remediation and discipline structures, drug prevention must start earlier. Contrary to what students sometimes claim, drug information is a factor in a student's resolve to stop using drugs. More typically, however, drug information, provided it is scientifically sound and appropriately cautionary, serves to fortify the resolve of those already disinclined to use drugs; but it is no less important for this fact.

An especially productive approach for high school age students has been (whether through health classes, biology classes, or through specially designed experiences) to introduce a comprehensive "model" of the psychosexual changes and intellectual changes associated with the period of rapid growth called adolescence, then to speculate, with students doing the synthesis, about the effects of various intoxicating substances on those crucial developmental processes. The necessity of adapting to stress should be emphasized, as should the recognizable personality losses that follow when normal adolescent stress management is modified by alcohol and other drugs which efface stress. In the teenage years especially, students will be able to call on their own experiences and observations to illustrate both healthy and drug-modified responses to adolescence.

No matter how complete and well-executed its programs of remediation, discipline, and prevention, day schools (and most boarding schools) cannot curb student drug use without organized, complementary activity from their parent body. Parents who have not yet begun to organize in response to student drug use might do well to make contact with the national parent organization in drug education, PRIDE, in Atlanta, Georgia. As in the orientation of a school faculty, parents need to be exposed to good information and to persuasive speakers: parents, physicians, educators. A self-appointed *ad hoc* steering committee of interested parents can provide, with school facilities and assistance, the early forums in which the incidence of student drug use is discussed as well as the obligation of parents to stop it.

When the awareness level is sufficiently raised, parents ought to be invited to sign a simple Agreement, pledging their cooperation and support for drug-free student activities and indicating a willingness to receive and to offer drug-related concerns to other parents who sign the Agreement. The parents who make this Agreement become in effect a Parent Awareness Network. A directory should be compiled of those who sign the Agreement, and from this pool officers and committee chairmen can be recruited.

The basic job of the Network is for members mutually to support one another in creating and then maintaining a drug-free climate for child development. Network activities include the formation of sub-networks by school grade level and even smaller networks consisting of parents of clusters of close friends. Household policies, curfew hours, and other parental expectations can be shared and discussed informally among sub-network parents as they see fit. Members and member groups should also extend Network activities outward: to adjacent Networks, to local merchants, to the press, to law enforcement and political bodies. Members should not lose momentum, either, if they are criticized as being "over protective" or "fanatics." Critics should be cheerfully but firmly asked to point out specific harms resulting from "excessive" concern over drug use and to weigh them against the past two decades' losses in student competence, family solidarity, school morale, and the health and life expectancy of young drug users.

Ultimately—and perhaps ideally—national political controls may curtail the cultivation, manufacturing, and distribution of drugs of abuse. But there are two dynamic pathways to such an outcome: from the top down and from the bottom up. For whatever reasons, the drug epidemic is not at the moment being successfully curbed in this country from the top down; there are already bright signs, however, that wherever a grass roots school and parents movement to prevent drug use has taken hold, it has been dramatically effective. So, "from the bottom up" looks to be the way out of the drug epidemic. It is not an easy way, but in compensation, the lessons learned through inventing local responses and hammering out local processes are humane and lasting lessons: "democratic" in the best sense. Once again the important thing is to begin.

Here in review is a suggested program of action steps, the chronological sequence of which may vary depending on steps already taken by a school:

— *Discover an "energizer,"* a persuasive agent of change. Introduce the "energizer" to the community served by the school in parent forums, student assemblies, faculty workshops.

— *Distribute printed information* to parents and faculty; build a drug education collection for the school's library reserve.

— Earliest drug prevention advocates, if not school administrators, must *win administrative and school board support* for a self-conscious initiative to curb student drug use: specifically, to *create a drug-free school*.

— *Train interested staff and faculty* to form a Core Group who with other faculty will coordinate and monitor drug-related student concerns, confront suspected users, convey concerns to families, refer chronic drug users to treatment, supervise reintegration of recovering drug users.

— *Revise school rules* and disciplinary procedures so that the severest consequences—dismissal from school, where allowable—follow first (and any) detected violations.
— *Devise a sequential program of drug education/prevention* experiences from the primary grades through the high school.
— Encourage and provide facilities for the *formation of a Parents' Awareness Network.*

No school's drug prevention program need be in whole or even in part like any other school's. The structure of a school's response should be shaped by whatever is workable for it in light of the goal: to create and to maintain a drug-free school. School life ought never to be about drug prevention. School life is necessarily about intellectual, physical, and character development, about arts, sciences, languages, and literature: the acquisition of the culture in a humane, stimulating setting. Creating a drug-free school is not the central business of education, but until a school is drug free the transmission of the culture will be impaired, and the school atmosphere will be distrustful and demoralized. Confronting the culture of drug use therefore has become an educational priority which cannot be ignored.

PART TWO:
A STORY

1.

THE ADVENT OF DRUG USE: THE SETTING

Reading the first part of this book—"The Concept"—it is possible to come away with two misleading conclusions. The first is that, once implemented, such a multi-dimensional program, involving school personnel and policies at many levels, is bound to work. No structured solution is "bound to work" against drug use. Drug use has two very powerful supports in its favor: (1) that the drugs themselves act on the brain's primary reward system, the very system which builds behavior and (2) that confronting drug use involves, at least initially, giving and getting very bad feelings, which most people try to avoid. In the face of these pro-drug supports, no "program" is guaranteed to prevail. The success or failure of any effort to counter drug use stands on the values of those who take on the fight and on the endurance of their commitment. The second misleading conclusion is that, given the societal supports for drug use, given the pleasurable reinforcement they deliver, and given the difficulties in mobilizing a school staff to do anything, the program described is bound to fail. This is demonstrably not true even in schools which have just begun to organize themselves to become drug free. Moreover, like the defense of pointing a blaming finger toward an ideological adversary (repressive conservatives, permissive liberals) or toward cultural forces too big to control (culture-wide narcissism, technological advances which promote instant gratification), a school's collective throwing up its hands in the face of acting effectively does nothing to diminish the "drug problem." Student drug use has not gone away, although many of the youth-specific fads which originally accompanied it into national prominence have receded or disappeared. Schools able to build a consensus to become drug free can become drug free.

Schools unwilling to build such a consensus, or that feel it is more enlightened and "realistic" to control abuse and promote "responsible use" of mind-altering chemicals, will continue to face a protean "drug problem."

What follows is an account of the experience of one school (the writer's, hence forward "I") as its staff struggled to understand and then to respond effectively to "the drug problem." The story is hardly streamlined, but therein may lie its chief value to actual school staff and parents wondering how to get to even a muddled first step. We, the staff of University School's Upper School, an independent day school for boys, have made cardinal errors in confronting student drug use. I say this with assurance in that I have made a good many of these errors myself. We have also, however, put together a system of drug prevention that has born community-wide results, which has made school life substantially drug free, and which has begun to alter the climate of students' out-of-school life as well. At the moment, we have a firm policy of dismissing students for first or any detected use of drink or drugs at school or school-related events. We have a thoroughgoing series of drug education presentations required of all students. We have a trained Core Group of faculty who confront students who have been associated with or whose behavior suggests drug use. We refer some students and their families to treatment, we arrange the readmission into school of some recovering users, and we maintain a support group for them and for others seeking help remaining drug free. Most recently we have promoted (and then stood back to observe) the foundation of a school-wide Parents Awareness Network which in its first year has involved a sizable majority of the parent body. Not unrelated to these developments, schoolwide morale has been on balance upbeat for the past several years, the mood constructive. The athletic and extracurricular program of the school has never been more productive or more heavily subcribed. Serious discipline proceedings have been infrequent and, for the past several years, have NOT been dominated by drink and drug infractions. The dominant school issues this past year were the quality and rigor of academic courses, the feasibility of a student-enforced honor code, how to promote a more welcoming environment on the part of old boys for new boys, especially for minority students. In short, the focus of school life has become school life.

In spite of being an independent college preparatory school for boys, University School's experience with the drug culture has been, so far as I can tell, virtually indistinguishable from any school's, public or private, boarding or day, in any region of the country. When I joined the school's faculty in the fall of 1968, the Campus Youth Movement (there were at the time more Americans under than over twenty-five years old) with its counter-cultural vanguard had passed itself down from the burgeoning college campuses into the secondary schools. Whereas on the college campuses the focal issues were university regulations which restricted student freedom and everything that bore on the war being waged in Viet Nam, the schools were mainly infected with the former concern. Less confining curricula, an easing of required courses and the introduction of topical elective ones were the central educational policy issues. School time began to be given over increasingly to what had previously been non-academic activity: experiential workshops and retreats, non-academic "intersessions" between terms. Through the middle to late nineteen seventies at my school it was not uncommon to observe "English classes" in which pairs of boys, hand in hand, groped blindfolded through the corridors and then returned to a classroom for an undirected discussion of "feelings of helplessness," while next door another English class took turns video-taping each other followed by an undirected discussion of how it felt to be "on camera." I remember a lot of movies. Popular song lyrics became "texts." One ninth grade English teacher embraced the idea of a "student-generated" reading list, and his students generated *Jaws, Go Ask Alice*, and some skin magazines. There was a feeling afoot among many faculty—and *all* faculties seem to have been divided during the Sixties (1965-1974?)—that school was up for redefinition. Current educational authorities encouraged this. A.S. Neill's free school manifesto *Summerhill: A Radical Approach to Child Rearing* was reissued to booming sales. Paul Goodman's *Compulsory Miseducation of Children,* John Holt's *How Children Fail,* and Jonathan Kozol's *Death at an Early Age* and other passionate tracts against traditional schooling circulated through our faculty room. With a series of planning sessions and a flurry of paperwork and scheduling befitting the allied invasion of Normandy, we combined with other area schools for a day-long teach-in experience on human sexuality, featuring Mary Calderone. By unanimous consensus this produced only acute discomfort. On a dare, during a massive Questions-and-Answer period, one of our boys, to the rib-jabbing hee-haws of his seat mates, scribbled out a question, "How do girls masturbate?" and to everyone's great unease, Ms. Calderone answered it thoroughly. There was a similar teach-in day about Viet Nam, in which congressmen, clergymen, army personnel, and others spoke passionately from unrelated premises. Finally, there was a multi-school, multi-location confab on Women Today in which order broke down altogether. An image lingers of a ponytailed girl of perhaps fifteen, tearfully and stridently protesting to one of the speakers, "Well, I like boys, and I'm always going to like boys, and you can never change that!"

My students now ask me repeatedly, "What was it like in the Sixties," rather in the manner of turn-of-the-century lads asking their grandfathers about the Civil War. It's a question worth answering carefully, because some students want to embrace a romantically revisionist view of the period in which a New Youth with New Politics (to the strains of New Music) tried briefly but mightily to convert a commercial, smugly war-mongering society into a paradise of brotherhood and peace, but were brutally cut down by the Chicago police in 1968, with those remaining killed at Kent State in 1970. The casualties include Jimi Hendrix, Janis Joplin, Jim Morrison, Martin Luther King, Malcolm X, and Robert Kennedy. Is this exaggerated confusion? Ask some current adolescents about the Sixties.

For many of us, especially in the schools, it may be instructive to sift through the order of events, to reexamine cause and effect, to contrast the images that were most frequent in popular media to what actually happened. There was, to an extent, a New Youth, a "counter-culture," no doubt because of their unprecedented numbers in unprecedented concentrations on campuses. The Beatles did trigger a massive explosion of popular music, but their emergence preceded the political developments of the Sixties which they would later cautiously embrace ("Well if you go talkin' about destruction/Don't ya know that you can count me out" and "If you go carrying pictures of Chairman Mao/you're not gonna make it with anyone anyhow"). Both sexes grew their hair longer. Men sported side whiskers, mustaches, beards, ponytails—sometimes all at once. The "tribal love-rock musical" of the period was *Hair*. Personal inhibitions and external restrictions on appearance generally were eased. Sexual inhibitions and restrictions were eased also, but it is hard to document with what effect. In the space of three years, movie lovers learned to undress. Student battles against college-imposed parietal hours (strictly monitored visiting periods between men and women undergraduates) were won; unmonitored co-educational dormitories have come to replace them.

Politically, the facts don't always support the journalistic image of the age. There is a strong impression, due to newsworthy public demonstrations and the winsome eccentricities of the most vocal "yippies," that there was a resurgence of "radical" (leftist) politics. There were left-wing organizations (such as Students for a Democratic Society [S.D.S.]) on many campuses, and there still are. Some of the organizations are Marxist, some Maoist. The more personal liberation organizations of feminists and gay rights activists have become prominent, overall, in the aftermath of the Sixties youth movement, not as an integral part of it. In many forms, many of them vocal and newsworthy, Sixties youth opposed the draft. But there was little uniformity or common affiliation among those who actually fled the country for Canada and Europe—or even among those who claimed conscientious objector status. The great majority of youth between the ages of eighteen and twenty who were given the franchise for the first time in 1968 voted Republican. Their presidential candidate was Richard Nixon. Not all of American youth were on the Chicago streets in 1968 during the Democratic National Convention. The presidential candidates (after Robert Kennedy was killed) whose campaign relied most heavily on youth movement support, Eugene McCarthy in 1968 and George McGovern in 1972, failed to galvanize the convictions even of the nation's youth.

So if there is a Sixties legacy to contend with, it is one which emphasized personal liberation rather than one of public reorientation. One badge of that personal liberation, one accepted from the outset of the Sixties youth movement, was the use of psychoactive drugs previously confined almost exclusively to the urban poor and to circumscribed "bohemians" in and about the performing arts. The Sixties message on drug use was emphatically favorable. The "political" voices of Sixties youth, such as Jerry Rubin's and Abbie Hoffman's, said *Do it!* (a commercially successful anti-commercialism book by Rubin, now a market analyst). The most commercially aired music also said, "do it": The Beatles sang, "I'll get high with a little help from my friends," The Birds sang *"Eight Miles High,"* and soon drug references became obligatory in rock repertoires. Documentary films like *Woodstock* showed widespread drug taking at youth festivals, and popular commercial films like *Easy Rider* began to feature pot smoking attractively. Timothy Leary, the press's most favored guru of drug use, then fresh from an association with Harvard University, proclaimed a new psychedelic age and urged the nation's young to "turn on, tune in, and drop out."

Marijuana, in preparations a tenth to a hundredth as potent as those available today, became the "warbreaker" drug: the "controlled substance" first tried by youth and the first to make its appearance in the entertaining of open-minded adults. Marijuana use became so ubiquitous that statutes against its use were unenforceable—or were at least unenforced—in public places where youth gathered, including college campuses. Marijuana use provided a stimulating "outlaw" context for the use of other drugs, at first mainly other hallucinogens: LSD, peyote, mescaline, psilocybin. Very quickly, however, in keeping with the patterns of drug use recognized long before the Sixties and since, drugs of every and any type made their way into the new youthful drug commerce. The generic name "drugs" became standard for what kids were "into." In this regard it is instructive, but painful, to witness the sessions in drug treatment centers in which children tell their parents, for the first time, their "drug histories"; even very vigilant parents who were convinced their child had a "pot problem" or a "drinking problem" learn that there has been multiple abuse. This behavior syndrome is confirmed by national survey data showing that the introduction of any new drug of abuse over the past twenty years has not substantially replaced the use of any other. The pool of illicit drugs seems to be one in which it is possible to add but not subtract.

But the most instructive lesson to be drawn from a consideration of psychoactive drug use in its Sixties' context is that while other emblems of the period have faded or disappeared—it is now more modish to have very short than very long hair, political activism is a muted phenomenon on campuses, colleges and schools are busy restoring the requirements they discarded a decade earlier—drug use has taken hold. More than that, it has spread out: both older and younger users have been recruited. The "campus" phenomenon of the middle sixties has become a standard feature of middle school (preteen and early teen) life. The "establishment" lambasted by Sixties' voices is now as apt to be composed of "recreational" (their word) cocaine sniffers and pot smokers as drinkers of cocktails. A newsworthy and swashbuckling automobile entrepreneur stakes his career on a multi-million dollar cocaine deal. The sensational press coverage of an exclusive girl's school headmistress accused of murdering her lover reveals that as she exhausted herself prosecuting pot smoking students, she herself had become dependent on prescription amphetamines. Movie heroes, sports heroes, and children of them have been associated with illicit drug use. So what's the big deal? This morning's *Boston Globe* carried a UPI article, dateline Los Angeles, reporting that psychedelics—LSD, peyote, and mushrooms—were on the rise again. The west coast phenomenon was expected to move eastward. A research pharmacologist is quoted as saying these drugs are produced now with fewer impurities and therefore there will be fewer "bad trips" (the assumption being that the "impurities" in the drugs cause bad trips) and that kids trust these psychedelics because the past decade's experimentation with them produced "no harmful effects." That was this morning.

The "big deal" persists mainly where the effects of drugs cannot be dismissed or denied: in families, in treatment centers, and in schools. From the outset of their widespread use and wherever they continue to be used, drugs affect and alter the lives of users and the life of the institutions composed of users. When student drug use became a factor in University School's life, school changed. It changed in what will be no doubt recognizable directions. What follows is my personal charting of those changes, concluding with our responses to them.

The school, whose faculty I joined in 1968, was a good, traditional example of its type: an academically rigorous, athletically distinguished (perhaps arts-deprived) preparatory day school, most of whose graduates were and still are admitted to highly selective colleges and universities. The school's traditions included that boys wear coats and ties (in combination with other clean and presentable clothes), that they attend a formal morning assembly (no longer a "chapel" with prayers and hymns), that they dine "family style" at tables presided over by faculty members, called "masters," even if they were women (direct address to faculty was usually "sir," and one woman teacher reported, with deep satisfaction, that she was addressed once as "Miss sir").

By 1968 drugs had begun to make an impact on the lives of our upperclassmen. Specifically, opportunities to use marijuana and, more rarely, LSD were presenting themselves on weekends. The access to these drugs initially was through older brothers on college campuses. But within two years, school-aged boys had themselves forged direct links to drug suppliers in greater Cleveland. At this point in-school drug use or intoxication at school and at school events was, if it occurred at all, so negligible as to be thought non-existent. The boys continued to go through the familiar motions (not familiar, however, to me, new on the job), but some of them had learned to get high and were enthusiastic about it. These way-breakers into illicit drug use were, moreover, some of the most accomplished and attractive boys in the school. At this point, too, drug use was still decidedly "politicized," occupying a place somewhere between the liberal left and the pop anarchism of the Yippies. Some of the advance scouts into drug use liked the "anti-establishment" dimension of their getting high; it provided extra support for what they, at the nub, felt a little guilty and scared doing. There were some other factors that shaped this early environment of drug experimentation. One was that some of the younger faculty smoked marijuana themselves; one in particular was a chronic smoker and had become badly muddled in consequence. As it happens, I was not among them. Although my undergraduate college had become thoroughly suffused with drugs (mainly marijuana) by my senior year, and while at graduate school in Cleveland pot had become standard at social gatherings, drugs just missed drawing me in. Looking back, three things combined to steer me, if not clear, at least around the outskirts of drugs: (1) a conviction instilled in me as a boy by my family, school, and church that drugs (all called "dope" in the cautionary school films) were horrible, (2) being very busy, and (3) the extreme tedium I found in the company of stoned people. But I digress. Some of the young faculty smoked pot and found ways of letting on that they did so (not to senior faculty or to the headmaster), and this, while it was never thrown up in anybody's face, probably contributed to the ambivalence students felt in making their own drug decisions; in a few instances I remember this was certainly the case.

Another factor affecting the particular early drug climate in which our boys moved was the level of social drinking in the community. The relatively prosperous suburbs on Cleveland's east side, from which a majority of our students still come, has always, so far as I can tell, been a hard-drinking region. Until recently, the parental views about middle to older teenagers drinking beer and other alcoholic beverages was not even ambivalent; there was a tacit (although never unanimous) consensus that it was fine. Some parents expressed the feeling that boys will be boys, and winked at drinking bouts, including the invariably dramatic "bad drunk." These were assumed to be part of the adolescent rite of passage, even providing hilarious and deeply rooted fraternal bonds. This, when articulated, tends to be a father's view. Mothers, at least some of them, are inclined to think that precocious drinking is attractively sophisticated—especially when the boys are dressed in evening clothes, as indeed they are for the poshest of club affairs and for all occasions organized around the presentation of debutantes. And again, this is not a recent phenomenon. School trustees, who have had grandsons graduate from the school, have told me that mixed drinks were served to them in the standard course of their out-of-school social life when they were students in the twenties and thirties. Without question the stories told most energetically when school alums assemble for annual dinners include those featuring some especially outrageous stunt or disaster perpetrated while someone was blind drunk.

Not all of this drinking lore is confined to the realm of nostalgic recollection. Substantial numbers of the school's graduates have proceeded on to confirmed syndromes of alcoholism. Some are recovering, some not; others are dead. The school's alums are also multiply represented in the dozens of AA meetings organized all over Cleveland's east side. A few of the meetings are dominated by University School people, an observation whose appearance is not, I know, in the spirit of the anonymity rightfully insisted on by AA, but which I nevertheless feel makes an important point. At one meeting site in particular, University School students and graduates, ranging from 14 to 70 years old, belong. Some of them, to their enduring credit, have become central figures in alcoholism and drug abuse prevention in the city.

So there was a climate not unfavorable to intoxication before the advent of the new, illicit psychoactive drugs of the Sixties. Moreover, and perhaps inevitably, intoxication caused periodic school concerns. Some of the behavior that followed adolescent drinking parties, especially the large, open, unchaperoned ones at commodious residences when somebody's parents were out of town, could not be ignored by the community or the school. As a characteristic of drunkenness generally, behavior at the big parties could be abusive. Sexual irresponsibility was reported, drivers ruined vehicles, got hurt, a few lost their lives.

A school's controlling out-of-school behavior is always difficult. Private schools, however, make a contractual arrangement with the families of the students they enroll, and on this account they have more latitude than many realize about what behaviors they can specify as conditions of enrollment. For instance it is legally possible to specify that drinking or stealing at any time, on or off campus, may result in a student's dismissal. The problem in doing so is enforcement. A school's staff only occasionally finds out about rule infractions outside school. Parents typically set themselves against sharing information with a school likely to use that information to dismiss their children or the children of friends. Parents may share concerns and information about student problems if they have a strong consensus about the seriousness of the problems, but as I have said, there was no such consensus at work in the community. In the face of this, our school's headmaster drafted a statement that walked a rather precarious line between the school's in-school and out-of-school jurisdiction. The statement was occasioned by yet another notorious instance of the "uncontrolled party syndrome" and was entitled "Where We Stand." This statement reminded parents that drinking was forbidden for students at school events and that drinking out of school was against the state law. It also made reference to legal precedents which had held host parents (whether actually in attendance at their homes or not) financially and legally liable for mishaps which befell underage drinkers on their premises. The statement concluded that the school, like the law, reserved the right to hold host families specially responsible—and subject to school action. What action was not specified. Perhaps for a time after its circulation, the parent body was more on its guard about allowing student drinking revels, but in fact instances of the forbidden sort of party occurred, and the school was not made aware of them. Occasionally, the school was aware of them, but was hesitant to act. Actually, and unsatisfactorily, the situation at the advent of youthful drug use was that the school wanted its students to obey the laws and to respect the in-school prohibitions against drinking, while standard community practice was to allow drinking in some settings while remaining oblivious to it in others. School and community combined to present students with a perfectly ambivalent atmosphere in which to make their "partying" decisions. And this is quite another thing from the eternal ambivalence every emerging adolescent experiences between what he feels like doing and what he knows he is supposed to do. Here there were genuinely mixed messages about what one was supposed to do. Adult ambivalence is

The Advent Of Drug Use

translated by an adolescent as "they don't know." In a decision field in which "they don't know," adolescents do what they feel like doing. University School adolescents at the dawn of the Sixties felt like getting together in the least confining circumstances they could find and drinking. Some of them felt like getting drunk. Some of them felt like trying drugs.

The students who first began using drugs in the late Sixties moved between two irreconcilable worlds. At school they were still expected to—and did—work hard for scholastic and athletic recognition, still wore coats and ties, still addressed their "masters" as "sir." The surroundings, the feelings, and the behavior connected with drug use bore no relation to school life at all. These early drug experimenters, like those experimenting today, didn't immediately display the now-familiar signs of drug-using youth: dishevelment and being chronically underdressed or inappropriately dressed; the alternately "wired" and bemusedly "laid back" bearing; the curious shift to a center part in one's hair; performance skids and lapses. From my perspective as a beginning faculty member trying to manage my duties, these were my "first" students; I assumed they had always been that way in Cleveland. And, as Bob Dylan sang at the time, "The times they are a-changin'." I supposed high school students would follow suit.

2.

EXPERIENCING STUDENT DRUG USE: THE EXPERIMENT TAKES HOLD

The "drug problem" became an official part of the school's history when, over a decade ago, the exchange of some marijuana in the student parking lot was detected and came up for disciplinary action. As the facts came out (not necessarily completely or accurately), it appeared that a boy who had some marijuana in the glove compartment of his car let two other boys know it. These two then arranged to purchase some of the first boy's supply. The exchange was observed by another student who told his friends, who then told their friends, one of whom let on to a teacher, who informed the school's administration. Confronted with the alleged transfer, one of the three boys involved admitted it, which led to reluctant admissions from the other two. A hastily assembled *ad hoc* faculty committee was formed to consider a response to this novelty. Suddenly it all seemed very serious: drugs. There was no specific written school rule against drug use or exchange at the time, although drinking was a clear violation of school policy, and, one assumed, drugs must surely be worse. The disciplinary response was fairly stiff: one boy was dismissed and the other two were suspended for the few weeks remaining in the school year. The decision was based on a distinction about which we have since had serious doubts: that the boy who had come to school with the pot was more at fault than those who purchased it. The distinction rests on the sensible logic that if no one brought drugs to school, there could be no use, exchange, or purchase. But for the supplier, some reasoned, the two purchasers would have proceeded to their cars and home for dinner. Against the receiver-supplier distinction, however, is the fact that the receiver (buyer) is often the initiator of the exchange, urging someone who has, or has access to, the forbidden substance to bring it to school. The distinction also helps to confirm the very arguable assumption that a boy offered something illegal and obviously inappropriate by another student has an understandable difficulty resisting the offer. The supplier-receiver distinction and its underlying assumptions would be reconsidered later.

In the aftermath of the "incident" and the disciplinary response to it, everyone at school felt bad. Serious school discipline almost always raises jittery feelings among the student body if it is, like ours, small enough that everybody can in principle know everybody else. The students felt bad, and they let us know it. They let us know, among other things, that the boys caught were small potatoes compared to some others they could (but would not) name. The idea that this incident was a "tip of the iceberg" was not pleasing to a faculty many of whom would have been sufficiently appalled if the parking lot violation had been the whole iceberg. Then, too, there was the minority of younger faculty, some of them "into" pot themselves, who felt the school had acted hysterically. The boy who had been relatively straightforward in the disciplinary proceedings was castigated strongly by other students for "Narc-ing."[10] Although he was invited to, he chose not to reenroll in the school after his suspension. The families of the boys in trouble revealed the usual mixture of feelings: embarrassment, worry, resentment at the school for laying such a "mess" at their feet. Finally, the administration, as I have since learned to know well, was buffeted back and forth in the currents of bad feeling generated by the three sets of hurt and angry parents, by a worried and critical faculty, and by an apprehensive and ornery student body. School trustees were starting to ask, "Is there a drug problem in the school?"

Although in the seven or eight years (a lot of school!) to follow, there would be an unbroken rhythm of disciplinary events of this kind, each in its way draining and demoralizing for all parties, the main impact of student drug use was experienced in the behavior of students who did not get caught. Whatever the actual incidence of drug use in the early to mid-seventies (for our purposes the zenith of the "Sixties"), it is almost certainly true that a large majority of our students had tried pot and/or another illicit drug, in addition to alcohol, while enrolled in the Upper School. A number of for-

[10](literally, "behaving like a 'narc,' or narcotics agent," in this case coming clean and implicating others; a drug culture word).

mal and informal surveys confirmed as much. Such are the liberties and mobility granted to contemporary teenagers that it was possible to acquire and use drugs regularly—even daily—without actually having to use and exchange them at school, although some students did this too. It was over the tip of the latter iceberg that the school's disciplinary system occasionally grazed.

What none of us could avoid, though some tried mightily, were the significant changes in the students we taught, coached, directed, and counseled. Since the nation had been through tumultuous times and there had been a documented youth movement, many of the faculty hypothesized that perhaps nothing had "happened to" the old model of student; rather, a new model had been produced by "rapidly changing times." While never quite articulated in those words, that was the thesis hammered out and argued over through hundreds of hours of student report meetings. We began to accommodate the epidemic of youthful drug use. And since drugs change users, and since we were accommodating those changes, drug use changed all of us.

Very frankly, few of us saw much student drug use (nor did we want to see it). What little each of us did know about came to us through our closest advisees. As it turns out, many of us now seem to have been privy to different pockets of drug abuse which we knowingly assumed to be all of it. More critically, faculty aware of any student drug use at all, even when the user was physically and emotionally close to collapse, did not assume that drugs were causal to the disturbing behavior we saw, but rather that drug use was a symptom of problems at home, such as being barred from using the car. Again, if the "counter culture" had produced a new kind of person, perhaps our traditional expectations did not apply; perhaps they were the problem.

This new kind of teenager produced by the age tended to present himself to us in his "new" incarnation in September, after the summer vacation. The transformation of one particular boy is especially memorable. A rather agreeable, typical "preppy" sort of boy, he came back to us in the fall of his senior year with long hair cascading over his shoulders in the manner of a pre-Raphaelite beauty. Our published school guidelines on appearance include the statement, "Hair should be neat and clean and worn well off the shoulders." The director of the Upper School called the boy into his office and told him in a hearty, cajoling sort of way that the cascading tresses had to go. The boy froze. "If I have to cut my hair," he said, "I am going to kill myself." His manner suggested he meant it. The counterproposal gave the director serious pause, and he shared the problem with some of the rest of us on the faculty. A thorny issue, we agreed—how far did we really want to go with this hair standards business? A "compromise" was reached; the boy was allowed to keep his long hair, provided he wore it either in a tight ponytail, the tail part of it tucked under his back collar, or in a tidy French twist held fast by bobby pins. So we solved that problem.

But there were tidal waves of others. The three-year math requirement had emerged, for the first time in the school's history, as an insurmountable obstacle to some students' graduation. Couldn't the requirement be waived, wondered sympathetic faculty on the humanities side of the curriculum? Some students have a math block, it was explained. A similar block was soon identified for the less apt foreign language students struggling to meet that graduation requirement. Paper-writing blocks and test-taking blocks emerged to plague other disciplines. To better address these "blocks" and to ease debilitating "pressure" (such was the academic mood that no one even bothered to confirm that the "pressure" was being experienced despite a lighter writing and reading load than was assigned a decade earlier), English and history classes began to drop an instructional day per week in favor of a "conference" day, a "reading" day, or just a day off.

There was at the same time a series of faculty meetings which focused upon the issue of whether black students should be allowed to have moustaches (this too in opposition to stated school appearance guidelines). Two passionate faculty camps arose, both of them white, on each side of the issue. There was no opposition to the proscription on moustaches *per se*, just on black students' moustaches, the claim having been put forth that by depriving a black student of a moustache, he was being deprived of a cultural norm. Voices rose, tempers flared. I honestly cannot remember if any students were interested in the issue, though some wore tentative-looking moustaches (they were hard to prosecute, in light of the hair "compromise" already made). The moustache-for-blacks issue was finally resolved when the exasperated proponent of the "cultural norm" thesis dramatically left a faculty meeting and reentered with an issue of *Ebony* magazine from the school library. "Here," he said. "Count how many black men don't wear moustaches." We did: about half wore them, half didn't. The issue lost immediacy. Student appearance remained about the same: eccentric and decidedly ratty.

With hindsight it is now clear that this was a drug-riddled period in the school's history, also in the nation's history. But it should not have required hindsight; students were laying their drug use virtually at our feet. I have mentioned some of the disciplinary infractions. Poems in the school's literary magazine were larded with veiled and not-so-veiled drug references. One talked of moving through a weekend haze of "sweet smoke and gin." A student skit at Christmas time substituted the following line in an enactment of *The Night Before Christmas.*

Away to my window I flew in a flash
Threw open the shutters, tore into my stash.

In a creative writing course I taught at the time, I was continually impressed with the frequency of drug references in the personal narratives, poems, and especially in the humor my students submitted. An even more telling, if also more subtle, sign of drug use on the part of those we knew to be involved was a lack of development and of substance in written work. A certain kind of drug-using student, invariably pot smokers, seemed to grow simple before one's eyes.

I have mentioned (with a reflex cringe of embarrassment) that we "knew" about some students' drug involvement. We tended to know about it through individual counseling conducted with students and their families or through actual infractions of school rules, detected but not confronted. One boy, who after a tumultuous career with us developed a serious and self-acknowledged drug problem in college, came back to school to talk to me about it. After he disclosed the (considerable) extent of his drug use while at school, I asked him how he managed not to get caught. He told me he did get caught, several times by his parents and once at school. The incident at school had occurred in the course of a school dance. He had periodically ducked out of the dance (also against school rules) to smoke pot behind the school buses at the rear of the school. Heading back into the dance, he was hailed by a teacher, a good friend of mine, who had seen the boy lighting up. There was a confrontation, during which my friend reportedly told the boy, "How stupid can you get—do you know you could get kicked out for this?" Yes, the boy did know. My friend decided to keep the incident "under his hat" and, as the boy's parents subsequently did, let it go with a warning. The boy, whose education, employment, and personal relationships to date have been riddled with drug-related crises and disappointments, told me he would always be grateful for my friend's leniency: "I don't know what I would have done if he turned me in."

My benighted friends and colleagues weren't the only problem. I can also recall an incident from the same early seventies period when heading out the school's long driveway on a crisp October afternoon, I stopped my car to offer a lift to two tenth graders who were ambling along the grassy shoulder of the drive. Once they were in the car, it was clear something was wrong with them. Normally exuberant boys, they were muddled and hesitant of speech; moreover, their clothes were pungent with the growingly familiar odor of pot smoke. I drove on for a while, testing my impression, then turned the car up a driveway, stopped it, and faced them. "I don't know what you guys were doing in the fields along the drive," I said. "But you smell like pot to me." There was great discomfort, but no denial. "Well," I said, "If I ever learn that you guys are smoking pot, there's going to be trouble." With the unfailing clarity of hindsight, I realize that I not only failed to ask them if they had been using marijuana, I also did not attempt to confiscate their supply. I drove on. Neither boy graduated from the school. One was dismissed for academic failure, the other for an unexplainable cessation of all school work and chronic truancy.

We prided ourselves then, and still do, on our counseling capacity. Besides deans and a few specialized guidance people, every faculty member serves as a faculty sponsor (advisor) to students who elect him or her early in the school year. Some teachers have a couple of sponsees, others as many as a couple of dozen. While not strictly circumscribed by policy, it has always been the practice that some measure of student-teacher confidentiality is possible in this relationship. Because communication is close in many of these relationships, drug use was discussed as openly there as it would be discussed at all across generations. One of my faculty friends, a clergyman, was a very popular teacher and perhaps our most heavily elected sponsor. In a conversation with him about one of my students (his sponsee) who was behaving oddly (occasionally not responding to direct questions, acting vague, doing little work), he asked if I could keep a confidence. I said I would. The confidence was that the boy was a regular pot smoker. I marveled that my friend knew all about it—how much the boy smoked, where he got it, with whom he smoked, etc.

"Aren't you trying to get him to stop?" I asked. "I've told him what I think," my friend responded, "but that decision is up to him." He went on to explain the very precarious and depressing circumstances facing the boy at home: an alcoholic father, financial worries, and a disturbed younger sibling. The important thing my friend felt, and felt sincerely, was to keep communication open with the boy. For my part I felt increasingly uncomfortable in the confidential knowledge that this boy was passing, at least technically, through our midst in a state of visible anesthesia.

My friend's example as a counselor—in many respects a wonderful example—became the model of how I hoped to develop the counseling dimension of my work. My intuition, confirmed with each school day, that drug use was a real snag in my students' personal development, did not seem at odds with the primacy of keeping the lines of communication open. Within a year or two, I too had access to drug-related and other student confidences at which colleagues marveled. The time I was not teaching was increasingly spent in intense, confessional bouts with students. Drug use figured into nearly all of them. So heavy was the load and so specific the counseling role I had (enthusiastically) taken on, that the school facilitated what turned out to be a nearly ten-year training practicum with a gifted adolescent psychiatrist who served as consultant to the school. In time, I would set up counseling workshops for other of my colleagues interested in adolescent psychology and in counseling. This was a stimulating time, although the period overall represented something of a nadir in student achievement and morale. But we were getting to know students more thoroughly, more confidentially than we had ever known them before. Lines of communication, we believed, were open.

But one's counseling role could send students mixed messages: this teacher (bound to impart and uphold school rules) is accessible for talk about anything (including the violation of student rules, including dangerous and criminal conduct). We were convinced that this was not a true ambivalence—that respecting confidential admissions was not equivalent of approving the behavior admitted—but the student body and many of the faculty had a harder time figuring "where we were coming from." And in fact the dual roles of confidant and enforcer of standards could confound even those who professed them. I, for one, was confounded from time to time. One specially memorable instance occurred one night out at school while I was showing a feature-length film to a class of seniors. A quick head count before the first reel showed that one boy was missing. The missing boy, a sponsee of mine, was a serious concern. Erratic and volatile to the point of delinquency, he had disrupted his household to the point that his mother (divorced father lived elsewhere) had all but given up attempting to control him. One way or another, he took up a substantial portion of my days at school. Midway through the film, I was suddenly aware of him beside me in the darkened auditorium; he had to talk to me. We went outside. His story, as it unfurled, was harrowing. He had been over to a girl friend's house while her parents were away—a house in which he was under any circumstances unwelcome, as the girl was just thirteen, and he was seventeen. Apparently he had been the source of many particular problems there. At the house amorous intimacies had led to the girl's bedroom where the couple was dramatically interrupted by the girl's mother. Mayhem ensued. The boy told me that the woman had threatened his life, in fear for which he fled the house and began driving aimlessly through the suburban streets. In the course of this account it became undeniably clear to me that the boy had been smoking pot, must have been just smoking it. His breath, his hair, his parka reeked of it. I interrupted, "Have you been smoking pot?" "Yes," he said impatiently, "I needed to relax. It's been a crazy night." I remember going round and around trying to follow the boy's elusive narrative and to help clarify for him how it had become a crazy night. I did not confront his marijuana use as (1) a poor defense for his anxiety about the incident at the girl's house, (2) a contributing cause of the incident at the girl's house, or (3) a clear violation of school rules. Except to ask a question, I didn't confront it at all. (Nor, given my current experience of students' marijuana intoxication, would it have been very effective to have done so that moment.) I should have taken the boy home, talked to him and disciplined him later when he was sober. Although thoroughly "in touch with" this boy's behavior, habits, friends, his domestic situation, and his personal history, I was able to contribute nothing to stabilizing his behavior. Nor was the skilled adolescent psychiatrist, to whom I ultimately referred the boy able to help. What seemed to help was residential treatment for chemical dependency (pot the drug of preference) undertaken by the boy voluntarily when he was twenty-three.

In fact, the drug and alcohol treatment undergone by some of our graduates after they left the school combined with the tragic deaths of a few others, taught us a good deal about the "new kind of youth" we thought had been produced by the "age."

A fairly heated faculty dispute arose over what course of action to take in response to an unusually eccentric tenth grader. Up to the tenth grade he had been something of a faculty favorite: bright, warm, with a remarkably subtle, dry sense of humor. In tenth grade this picture changed. He would speak up almost randomly and a little crazily in class. Assignments would not come in—or they would be submitted in unacceptable form—a single cryptic sentence instead of a research paper, a rambling, stream-of-consciousness poem in the place of an exam. His dress went from ordinary to whimsical to bizarre, so that his standard turnout had become an outsized tuxedo, complete with cane and top hat. He received at least one "work squad" (work detail given for a routine discipline infraction) for dancing unrestrainedly through an academic corridor in this get-up. Some of us defended him vigorously as an agreeable eccentric, marching to his own drummer. This was, after all, the era of the surreal "happening," the golden age of incongruity (television's *Laugh In*, early *Monty Python*, *Firesign Theatre*, etc.). There was an honest reluctance to snuff out the essence of this sprite in the name of deadening conformity. In our faculty Report meeting (the same forum where the moustaches-for-blacks controversy had raged a year or two before) voices were again being raised: the tuxedo was, after all, within the school's stated dress code—if he could just be convinced to leave the top hat in his locker until . . . Nonsense!, stormed the opposition. The boy is putting on the dress code with that outfit. He is, moreover, calling distracting attention to himself in the process. He is as disruptive to a class or an assembly as someone without any clothes on at all. "What harm is dress, anyway?" someone would always contribute. Then one afternoon in the midst of these exchanges someone who knew the boy and his family well said, "I think what is happening is that _____ is taking a lot of acid, and he's out of control." To which somebody said, "If you know that's what's happening, you ought to do something about it."

As it happened nobody did anything about it, although the tuxedo was effectively banned. In less than a year, the boy's campy exhilaration was gone, and in its place was a syndrome of chronic tardiness, illnesses, and missed assignments. The boy still had his champions, however, and some of them resolved to give him credit for even the most divergent kinds of output. In his senior year, he managed to be able to take two of his four courses (an exceptionally light load requiring special faculty approval) as "independent study." The independent study courses were composed of a series of esoteric readings selected by the boy. In the end he failed to read many of them and found himself unable to write about them at all. On the basis of periodic tutorial discussions, he "passed" these courses and, upon graduation, was admitted to a highly respected undergraduate college. He dropped out of college his first year there and has drifted between psychiatric hospitals ever since. He was originally hospitalized for drug abuse (which his parents and therapists agree commenced in the tenth grade). His current diagnosis is acute and chronic schizophrenia out of which he arises for periods of relative coherence, provided he is medicated regularly with heavy doses of Librium.

A faculty friend and I often look back in wonder at our (and our colleagues') "counseling" during this period. We must have spent at least forty or fifty hours per week at it in addition to classroom and other duties. We met with irascible boys individually, with their families, a few times even with their extended families. Distinguished psychotherapists came to school to train us. Family therapists came in to work with us on family dynamics. We were run through listening and perception-heightening exercises. We worked on being "non-directive" in our counseling sessions.

No boy in our school's history, perhaps in any school's history, received more intensive or sheer hours of counseling than did a boy I shall call, for anonymity's sake, Paul. Paul first surfaced as a concern, as did the boy previously discussed, in the tenth grade. Before that he had established a mark for himself as a strikingly good-looking boy who was both a good student, with a fine ear for languages, and a promising soccer and tennis player. He was a sponsee and a language student of the friend mentioned above, and it was he who first brought up Paul as a school concern. After a ninth-grade year as what my friend called a "golden boy," Paul had gotten off to a poor start in the tenth grade. Daily work was not being done in any course, even in German and French where he could get by on natural facility. He didn't go out for soccer. He was whiny and irritable when confronted about these things. His parents—father and stepmother—réported that he was being very "uncooperative" at home. While technically within the dress code, he had begun to look disheveled and not quite clean.

In the course of the counseling which followed, including daily sessions with his sponsor and several weekly sessions with me, we learned quite a bit about Paul: his mixed feelings about his father, his unmixed resentment of his stepmother, his perhaps unfinished feelings about the death of his mother. One development that seemed clear to us was that the children in the family—an older brother and sister in addition to Paul—were allied strongly against the father and the woman he had married. We asked the brother and sister in to school and talked at length. The brother and sister seemed more accommodating of their stepmother than Paul did; they too were finding Paul inappropriate at home. We had the whole family in to talk further. The problem, in Paul's father's view (rather tentatively seconded by his stepmother) was that authority in the household had broken down; Paul did whatever he wanted. "Like what?" we asked. "Like refusing to keep household rules." "What rules?" There was an uneasy pause. "Rules about his damned pot equipment." Apparently Paul had been smoking pot openly at home, despite its being forbidden. His father said Paul's room stank of it. He said moreover that he had gone into Paul's room a number of times and found "equipment" (water-cooled bongs, "toking" scissors, hashish pipes), even after "equipment" detected earlier had been thrown out and expressly forbidden in the house. "Yeah!" exploded Paul, "You're always coming into my room without asking!" We had it, we thought: a problem in Paul's relationship to his father.

To our credit, I believe, my friend and I talked to Paul extensively about his pot smoking and urged him to stop. At one point I took pains to share some specialized research on the harmful biomedical effects of marijuana on the lungs, reproductive function, and the brain. These were fairly specialized medical journal articles clipped and interpreted for me by the psychiatrist with whom I was carrying on the practicum. In no way did Paul resist any of this; in fact, he seemed interested in the suggested medical and psychological effects of pot, many of which he acknowledged feeling. He did not, however, stop smoking marijuana, even at home. Health consequences aside, we told him, he was being both provocative and inappropriate smoking pot at home in opposition to his father's expressed wishes. To this Paul had no response.

Although I still saw Paul's behavior as pent up anger and defiance, not as a consequence of his drug use, I persisted in trying to get Paul to stop smoking pot. In the attempt, I tried a technique that has since never failed to be instructive, if not always effective by itself. Reasoning, I believe correctly, that every adolescent, even those who use drugs and who are otherwise delinquent, are attempting to maximize control, I asked Paul if he thought he was "in control of" his drug use or if it was in control of him? In other words, was he hooked? The question intrigued him, also, I think, scared him. Paul said he thought he was in control of it. "Good," I said, "but how about proving it by seeing if you can stay off pot and any other drug for a while, say, six weeks?" Paul said he really didn't want to do that—he liked pot—but he repeated that he was in control over its use. He also thought that six weeks was an unimaginably long time to abstain. I countered with four weeks. He thought this over. "Just to see if you are in control," I prodded. Paul agreed to try. But he failed. He didn't last three days. I found out about this in a surprising way. Another boy in Paul's class came to my office and asked to see me about something important. "Did you have a bet with Paul _____ about not smoking pot for a month?" he asked pointedly. I explained the arrangement to the boy, wondering the while how he knew about it. "Well," said the boy, "He didn't do it. He smoked up all weekend." What was this all about? I wondered. Why this behavior that looked like "narc-ing" from an emphatically unnarc-like boy. As it turned out, this boy and his friends were concerned about Paul, too. Even by the none too fastidious standards of their weekend "parties," Paul's pot smoking was aberrant.

But Paul could not see it this way. He assured me he could control his use, and tried the four-week abstinence again. And failed again. In this halting, very unproductive way, Paul's tenth and a good deal of his eleventh-grade year passed. His performance deteriorated steadily and dramatically. He looked ill and uncared-for. Once an immaculate, even vain "preppy," he rarely washed his hair, seemed never to change clothes, and he had allowed a textured deposit to form a film over his once-white teeth. His schoolwork was awful, and by his junior year he was on an academic probation which he showed no sign of being about to make. Late, inattentive, frequently absent due to illness and other complaints, he had lost any substantial connection to school life. An exasperated stalemate had been reached at home according to which Paul continued to smoke pot as he pleased, but received no communication beyond the practical minimum from his parents. As if to dramatize the desperation of his plight, Paul had three serious car accidents in two months and lost his driver's license indefinitely.

The program of his school counseling continued apace, yet Paul worsened, bouts of uncontrollable crying augmented his already alarming profile. A family therapist was recommended and tried by Paul's family, but nobody liked him, and the therapy ceased. The consulting psychiatrist to the school, a close friend and long-term mentor of mine, interviewed Paul and speculated that his pot intake alone could account for the behaviors we were seeing (with this diagnosis, the psychiatrist, Dr. Robert Gilkeson, may well have produced an historical landmark). Gilkeson had been for some time collecting specially administered electroencephalograms (EEG,) to chart neurological changes in his own pot-smoking patients. He felt Paul should be tested.

But Paul ran away. For several weeks he was a missing person, drifting around, as it turned out, the largely deserted summer communities of Cape Cod, returning when he was out of cash and other resources. An action step of some kind seemed essential. A number of us thought a boarding school might structure Paul's out-of-school life sufficiently to reverse his pattern of self-destructive behavior. With considerable effort and by appealing mightily to his promise before the tenth grade, I was able to get three or four reputable boarding schools to consider Paul, despite the past year's dramatic collapse. I had especially high hopes for one of the schools, a small New England church school where I knew some of the staff personally. But Paul was not admitted to any of the four, three of which turned him down on the spot (which is rare). As one might imagine, he did not interview well. At the school I preferred, the Dean asked Paul (quite rightly) if he was or had ever been involved with drugs. Paul did not deny it. The Dean then asked Paul if he would pledge not to use any drugs at the school, if it admitted him. Paul could not promise. That was that.

That would soon be that at University School, too, as Paul's grades were insufficient for him to reenroll in his senior year. Instead he went to his local high school through which he passed without much notice by taking language at competence levels he had already attained and by taking loosely structured electives in an alternative "school within the school" devised to accommodate the New Youth produced by the Age. For those at our school who knew him only slightly, it was something of a relief to see Paul go—

one less basket case to contend with. But for those of us who had invested hundreds of hours in probing, tearful, supportive sessions with him, Paul's loss seemed a profound and demoralizing defeat. Except that he liked us and would phone us periodically at home (he still phones us), we seem to have done nothing for him at all. Now in his late twenties, he lives supported by inherited money on the fringe of an academic community where he alternately considers a career as a professional interpreter, for which he is unqualified, and a career as a carpenter, for which he is also unqualified.

Paul was by no means the only source of demoralization as we moved through the mid-seventies. The frequency of major disciplinary cases had picked up, producing an unassignable sense of unease throughout the school. Students no longer seemed moved by the trappings of the counter-culture. "Hippie," and "radical" became terms of mild derision. An unsettling time: students were certainly not behaving themselves, but they were not misbehaving in the name of anything. Student judgment, both individual and collective, seemed, if anything, more unreliable than ever.

At times the sequence or coincidence of student problems ground ordinary school life almost to a halt. In consequence of one startling "incident" we came within an ace of expelling most of the junior class. The juniors had planned a large picnic for the Saturday afternoon following May S.A.T. tests. The party was to take place at a nearby farm, the facilities of which had been offered by a student whose parents owned it. When the parents heard about it, however, they had other views and forbade any such gathering in their meadows. Thus the students left the testing center early Saturday afternoon with all the preparations for a party—including several large trash barrels filled with beer—but no place to have it. Somebody suggested the school's athletic fields. The mood was such that the hilarity of this prospect—a beer party at school in broad daylight—overrode whatever cautions were expressed. School neighbors out walking their dogs, faculty joggers and tennis players—all manners of spectators noted and promptly reported the party, which was predictably loud and raucous. The juniors were assembled the following Monday morning as the rest of the school trooped off to classes. Many individual conferences followed, in which pointed questions were asked, most of them starting with "What could you have been thinking of to _____?" The majority of the class attended the party, and a quarter to a third of them were determined to have drunk some beer. The students seemed puzzled themselves at their judgment; their parents were exasperated. Many suspensions and probations followed, thoroughly souring that spring term. The junior class president, who attended the picnic but who did not drink, was castigated angrily by the school director. "You," he told the boy, "couldn't lead a fire drill!"

But if this was just spring shenanigans, boys being boys, etc., the accompanying incidents were not. A decidedly volatile student (drug abuse later confirmed) confronted the school director in the reception area and asked, for no specific reason, to be excused from a class. When the request was denied, the boy said, to a fairly wide audience, "Sir, why be such an asshole about this?" he was not disciplined for this; it was sensed, correctly, that he had a "problem." Exactly a minute after the two-week process of settling a major discipline infraction involving three underclassmen who had been caught planning to procure some marijuana, the phone rang in the headmaster's office where we were conferring. It was a faculty member in Washington, D.C., saying that several of the boys under his charge while on a study trip to the Capitol had been caught smoking pot in their hotel room and had been dismissed from the program. In the midst of this, I was called by the desperate parents of a junior who had seen a letter written by another student to their son threatening to have "some people who know how" hurt their boy physically, if he didn't pay up on a drug debt, the sum of which was staggering to the parents. In working through this unattractive mess with both families, I managed to find out exactly who the "people who know how" were. And through my none too pleasant discussions with one of them learned that one of the drug *sources* they dealt with was a member of the police department where one of the boys lived. This very same police department I had contacted for advice several times in the course of working through drug-related problems at school. The conversations always ran along the following lines:

I: "Well, we've discovered some boys at school in possession of _____. What do you recommend we do?"
Police: "Do you want to file a complaint?"
I: "Should we? Is that what you advise?"
P: "It's up to you."
I: "What do you usually do when this comes up? What do you do when you find some kids in the possession of _____?"

P: "We don't get much of that here."
I: "Well, if we file a complaint, what happens? How do we proceed?"
P: "You don't file it here. You file it with the department out where you are. That's if you want to prosecute."
I: "We want to get rid of these drugs at School."
P: "Why don't you just handle it yourself?"

Before this was resolved, a boy, the same boy who had recently addressed the school director with such surprising vulgarity, came pounding on his office window late one afternoon, desperate to see him. The boy was in a real panic. "What do you know about _____?" he said, referring to a friend of his. The director did know something about _____, as the headmaster of a nearby girls' school had just phoned him with the news that a number of girls there had just been "busted" for arranging to purchase drugs, including cocaine, from _____. The reason for his friend's panic is that he had just that moment read a suicide farewell from _____, indicating that he had been caught and was going to take his life rather than face the consequences. "Was this true? Had _____ been caught?" his friend demanded to know. The director called _____'s home and found out from the boy's father that, yes, his son had tried to commit suicide—he had swallowed insecticide from the family greenhouse—but that he was in the hospital and expected to recover.

The boy did recover. In some ways he recovered more quickly than we did. From my standpoint, the boy's crisis and near tragedy convinced me: this drug nonsense was taking a preposterous toll in student development, on faculty morale, and on the effectiveness of what was, at our best, a really fine school. Drugs were no longer a peripheral harm; they were central, polluting just about every element of school and community life. Enough was enough.

3.

UNDERSTANDING STUDENT DRUG USE

As I mentioned earlier, the counseling dimension of my work (I had since become Dean of Students, responsible for overseeing the school's guidance system) put me in regular weekly contact with our consulting psychiatrist, Robert Gilkeson.[11] Throughout the early and middle seventies our work dovetailed in what was for me a stimulating way. The routine for his school visits was for him to be available to faculty who wanted to discuss a specific student concern with occasional student interviews. After that, for an hour or two, he and I would run through my own work with students that week. Gilkeson has an ongoing fascination with the neurological foundations of experience—especially in identifying the neurological pathways of learning and other behaviors. Since a number of the students I was most worried about were involved with drugs, and since many of them became in consequence his private patients, he was able to establish a convincing model of the specific pathology caused by marijuana and other drugs and to explain to me and to others who would listen the relationship between the neurological actions of mind-altering drugs and the observable behavior of drug-using students we knew. He had been following laboratory research showing marijuana's effects on human and animal systems since the late sixties and was particularly interested in the work of Robert Heath and his associates in neuropsychiatry at Tulane. Heath's work located the actions of various drugs in deep sites in the waking brains of both monkeys and

[11]While Gilkeson's work on marijuana's effects on the nervous system is still in progress, he has reviewed it at several professional conferences and has shared some of it in popular magazine articles.

human beings; moreover, his studies showed damage in and between the neural cells affected.

Gilkeson was curious to have a clearer picture of what the cognitive gaps, slowed arousal, and poor memory—"spaceyness"—of his pot-smoking patients looked like neurologically, so he began, with their permission, to collect EEGs (brain wave recordings from electrodes placed about the surface of the scalp) from them. A "standard" EEG is normally administered to someone who has suffered an injury to the head or a stroke, and it is used sometimes as a diagnostic aid. In the standard EEG, the subject wired to the recorder is immobile and asked to relax; the graphed printouts from the various sites in the brain are then reviewed by specialists to see whether the frequency and contours of the recorded "waves" are within a "normal" range, measured in cycles per second. The "normal" range of an EEG can be misleading. It signifies to a neurologist the absence of certain pathologies, but it is not by any means an indicator of a person's "normality." In other words, a sampling of EEGs from the inmates of a high security prison would very likely fall within the "normal" range. Nor could the normal range of a standard EEG test reliably indicate the difference between an excellent and a failing student.

Gilkeson's work, which is ongoing, attempts to draw finer distinctions from EEG data than have heretofore been drawn. The EEGs he administers to patients[12] include both relaxed and attending states. When the subject has established a slow-wave or "relaxed" pattern, the person administering the EEG might ask a question ("Would you now spell your name backwards?"). The intention is to illustrate the differences in the pot smoker's and the nonsmoker's EEGs, showing the performance-related significance of differences within the "normal range." The interpretation of the electroencephalographs may seem highly technical and subtle, but the implications of Gilkeson's findings are profound and socially important. The preponderance of slow-wave activity, the delayed alerting response when questioned, and the frequent presence of irregular (pathological) wave activity in the pot-users' EEGs constitutes a syndrome one neurologist, a colleague of Gilkeson's, nicknamed "pot rot." This EEG pattern looks remarkably like the organic brain pattern of teenagers with severe learning disabilities. The seriousness of any drug-related loss of neurological function

[12]The subjects of his study have smoked pot twice a week or more for at least four months. They range in age from 16-20.

cannot be overemphasized, as neurological losses are not, strictly speaking, reversible; one may or may not adapt to them, but one does not "heal."

It was stimulating working with Gilkeson. By drawing comparisons to drugs like Ritalin® and Cylert® ; commonly prescribed in his field, he was able to demonstrate how a substance can block a sensation or an activity by facilitating other neurological activity that suppresses it; or, conversely, how a substance can seemingly *facilitate* activity by suppressing neurological controls over it. Seen this way, alcohol, which has the progressive effect of shutting down neurological activity unto death, can, along the way, shut down suppression of inhibitions, so that one feels, for a while, uninhibited, lively, "high." And of course a great deal of marijuana's appeal to youth lies in its ability to break down suppression. By suppressing sensory and other kinds of information, one can pay attention, make fine distinctions, discriminate. By breaking down suppression, all kinds of sensory and other information run together in a (perhaps pleasing) wash. If enough suppression is lost, even very elementary distinctions like "before" and "after" and "soon" cannot be made. When suppression is allowing one to discriminate, sensory information—say, a familiar tune—begins to trigger higher order mental functions such as associating the tune with former experiences in which it was heard, interpreting its lyrics, evaluating its quality. When suppression breaks down, the tune stops meaning and instead presents itself as raw sensory data. In this manner people under the influence of drugs which break down suppression often report "profound" elemental responses to familiar sensory experience, while in fact, at least neurologically, they have been temporarily stupefied.

It can be a tempting, very attractive thing to efface complexity in exchange for sensually pleasing here-and-now simplicity. It can be irresistibly tempting if, as is the case with many students in the years of their most accelerated development, the very attainment of complexity is an anxiety-provoking challenge. The retention, synthesis, and application of new mental operations is hard. One is only more or less gifted at it, or at parts of it. To use the philosopher Mortimer Adler's unequivocal terms, learning is achieved at the cost of pain. Not only is learning inherently stressful, the fruits of learning can be the cause of further stress. Being educated to see the world as it really is (ecologically) may not in itself be a pleasure. Nor is seeing one's family as it really is always a pleasing process.

Nor is oneself, on thorough and objective scrutiny, often an object of satisfying contemplation. For all that is said about it, learning development, seeing the relationship of parts to wholes, cause to effect, can be a great pleasure to turn off. And in a culture which holds pleasure above all things, that is exactly what will happen. Perhaps one of the most pernicious things about drug-altered people is that the critical capacity they need to understand what they are losing or have lost has been itself altered by drugs. Children who are in the process of acquiring that critical capacity are in a poor position to know and care about such losses.

Learning at every level requires one to store experiences in memory. Another thing Bob Gilkeson helped me to see was the neurological elegance of remembering and, perhaps even more important, the impairment to learning that results from interfering with memory. All mind-altering drugs interfere with memory. They do so both by blocking or distorting experience entering consciousness and also by blocking the process by which short-term memories are neurochemically synthesized into long-term memory. Drug users are usually aware of this inability to process information[13] while they are high, but they fail to realize the losses continue after the feeling of being high has passed. For one thing fat-soluble drugs, like marijuana and methaqualone (a prescription sedative known commercially as Quaalude®), do not quickly break down and metabolize out of the body, as water-soluble substances (like alcohol) do. Delta-9-THC, for example, the most psychoactive component of marijuana, has a "half-life" of from several days to a week in duration meaning that half the biologically active chemicals which acted on the nervous system to make a user high are still present a week later, half of that a week later, and so on. Thus a person who uses marijuana regularly, or even daily, is accumulating THC and other metabolites in his fatty tissue. But this, logically, cannot go on indefinitely. After a few months of regular use, the user will become fat-saturated with THC (and other chemicals stored in fat). At this point users are likely to change physically, to be, in current parlance, "burned out," "spacey," "wrecked," "blown away," "fried." In this condition drug users begin to change appearance and behavior. Because THC (and other

[13]With the exception of those who use stimulants, like cocaine or amphetamine. In the early stages of using stimulants, users often feel *enhanced* powers of concentration and clarity of mind—impressions not confirmed, but in fact contradicted by objective external observation.

psychoactive chemicals) is thought to damage the cellular sites where it is active and where it is stored, and because those sites include brain, lungs, reproductive organs, and other glands, changes produced by marijuana, while to outward appearance gradual and undramatic, become finally a serious health and developmental concern.

Both clinical experience and laboratory tests on animal and human subjects reveal diminished performance—slowing, delayed arousal, inability to sustain attention, inability to sequence steps—resulting from "street level" doses of marijuana and other illicit drugs. The functions impaired are the ones most critical to learning. Moreover, short-term experience not converted into stored experience through learning, may be unrepeatable and irreplaceable. This is especially likely if the organ of learning itself—the nervous system—is sufficiently altered.

The implications of drug use on the development of students I taught and knew well had by now begun to seem both obvious and profound. Yet I could find no one in my profession willing or interested in calling attention to them. Thus in the spring of 1978, I was granted a term off from school to explore and to develop, among other things, the relationship between drug use and adolescent development. In the course of this leave I was able to spend time in hospitals working with specialists, including Bob Gilkeson. Two kinds of tuition were especially helpful. The first was a professionally guided tour through the medical literature published over the past ten years on marijuana. Here I was able to read and to ask questions about the specialized work of Heath, Nahas, and others. The other was a concentrated short course in neurology and neurochemistry from Gilkeson and some of his associates at St. Luke's hospital in Cleveland. Through this study I was introduced to the elegance and complexity of "normal" neural functioning and was able to begin to understand the consequences of interfering with it by the use of toxic chemicals. The neural circuitry of being alerted to a command, of processing the command to auditory memory and to various centers of verbal associations, the referral of these associations to deep brain sites for emotional "evaluation," the referral to forebrain sites for planning and action, the innervation of a motor response—all of these health-critical and learning-critical operations were fouled by marijuana and other illicit drugs. If nothing else, I felt driven to go back and tell my students about the majesty of the nervous system they were polluting: billions of neurons, trillions of connective pathways between them, neural systems that suppressed function, systems that facilitated function, cells which only hear, cells which only see, cells which store only language, centers which register rage, fear, and ecstasy.

But perhaps the most enduring lesson was a simple one: that a neural cell functioning "normally" was, in effect, perfect. No medicine, no tonic, no drug could improve it: make it see, hear, feel better. Medicines and drugs can knock out cells which feel or cause them to fire their arsenal of neurotransmitters all at once—but cell function is not improved; if anything, it is likely to be damaged by organic reaction with "outside" chemicals. If any cell, including a neural cell, is changed by the action of a chemical, it is changed in the direction of damage. The damage may be accompanied by waves of sensual pleasure or by striking hallucinations, but it is nonetheless damage. If one hears a bell when there is no bell ringing, that means brain cells are firing without sufficient cause. That is a neurological mistake; that is damage. An epileptic convulsion is a sign of the same kind of damage, only in a motor, rather than an auditory location. Commercial films and other popular culture images and messages which represent poor neural functioning as attractive or, more typically, funny have co-opted the natural tendency to worry about it. Probably enough has been written about the societal impact of portraying drunks as funny and lovable. The fact that these portrayals utterly falsify what it is actually like having an unrecovered alcoholic in the family or, for that matter, in the room does not seem to diminish the popularity of these portrayals. *Arthur,* a recent commercial motion picture about the antics of a wealthy young man who drinks in a lethally alcoholic pattern, has, in the eighties, created an attractive new stereotype for youth.[14]

Marijuana smokers become quickly familiar with certain kinds of neurological misinformation accompanying their drug use: mild to quite serious feelings of persecution, hunger pangs although one is full of food, a disorientation in time. Film comedians Cheech and Chong play up the humor of being stoned in movies whose central premise is illicit drug use. Drug users extol the experience of hearing familiar music in a "new way" when they are high, but do not pause to consider that the drugs have broken down hard-won sophistication to the extent that structurally simplistic

[14] It is even possible, in Los Angeles, to make money by impersonating Arthur and delivering "Arthur-o-grams" to others.

monotonously repetitive music has become engaging. But there is a strong resistance on the part of drug users to considering their drug experiences as loss of function. Users insist that drugs are "harmless" (except for bad/adulterated drugs) or, alternately, make the danger of abuse part of a drug's appeal; after all, some of the greatest youth heroes go out that way: Jimi Hendrix, Janis Joplin, Jim Morrison, John Belushi. The combined effects of the commercial promotion of drug highs, the tendency to deny their chronic effects, the glorification of their acute effects, and, finally, their capacity to prevent users from perceiving drug-connected losses create a considerable barrier against taking in bad news about drugs. Nor is bad news easy or desirable or even, in some social circumstances, safe to bear.

It is, however, still bad news. And those who take up the profession of education have got to bear it, if we are to do our job properly. Developmentally, children are supposed to become capable of increased function as they pass into adolescence. They are supposed to come to personal and social terms with their emergent sexuality. They are supposed to manage increasing amounts of unsupervised time and increased personal mobility in a responsible way. They are supposed to pass from more concrete to more abstract modes of thinking—from arithmetic to algebra, from "what happens" in a story to the meaning of the story, from familiar operations to the theory of what makes the operations work. They are supposed to learn to form mutually satisfying relationships with friends and lovers. They are supposed to scan the field of possible vocations and align their interests and talent with promising ones. In other words, like the neurological apparatus that enables these processes to occur, adolescent development is itself elegant and complex. It cannot happen without a capacity to endure stress, to strive. Development is the consequence of activity, often triggered by challenges, the goal of which is mastery. Mastery of a physical or mental operation is a source of profound pleasure. This sort of pleasure may have no sensual dimension at all, may even be, as in the case of the marathon runner at the finish line, accompanied by physical pain. Seen this way, development is the exact antithesis of drug taking. The drug experience breaks down function, slows activity and may even replace it altogether. And because psychoactive drugs carry the chemical capability of rewarding loss with profound sensual pleasures, they can be—and are to many—irresistible. They are most likely to be irresistible in a society that does not clearly commend the pursuit of mastery and development over the pursuit of sensual gratification.

This, at any rate, was how it seemed to me as I combined my researches into drug effects with a longstanding inquiry into the process of adolescent development. In that spring of 1978, while my colleagues at school were toiling "in the trenches," I put some of these thoughts down in a longish essay-argument titled "Some Unsettling Thoughts about Settling in With Pot." With no specific audience in mind, I showed a draft of the manuscript to some physicians, including Bob Gilkeson and Gabriel Nahas in New York, for technical review, and I gave a copy to my headmaster to let him know what I was up to. With other researches still ahead of me, I took off for Great Britain for six weeks to visit schools there.

While I was away, the school experienced what may in retrospect have been our definitive "drug incident." For the preceding several years our junior class had combined with the junior classes of two nearby girls' schools for a weekend retreat. Using the cabins and facilities of a state park nearby, these retreats had been highly praised by faculty and students alike for their success in combining serious discussion with informality. Student leaders from the three schools met periodically throughout the school year to organize the program: group sessions with a psychologist facilitator, games which stressed group cooperation, films, skits, a square dance, shared chores. The planners of the '78 retreat decided that the central theme should be "Trust."

The retreat was heavily subscribed. Before departure some obligatory words were said to our juniors about hours, about not bringing alcohol and drugs to the state park, and about other procedures. The collective mood was jubilant, the May weather glorious. Thereafter disaster ensued. The warnings about alcohol and drugs were not heeded. In fact, as it turned out, fairly elaborate advance plans were made to bring beer, wine, marijuana, marijuana paraphernalia, and some other drugs to the retreat. Faculty chaperones, many of whom were given only a cursory outline of their responsibilities, were bewildered that students were so long returning to their cabins after the planned evening activities. One of the younger, more savvy chaperones returned to her cabin to fetch her cabin mates missing from the square dance and found the cabin empty but pungent of pot smoke. The structured activities fell flat. The recommended curfew and inter-cabin visiting policy were ignored. At any given moment, especially after dark, it was hard to determine where everybody was.

Where they were, many of them, was in the woods, in small and large clusters, passing bottle and joint. The retreat had become a "party" the momentum of which grew to the extent that students on retreat telephoned out (in violation of stated guidelines) to other students to drive out to the state park and join in. Several students did, including some from non-participating schools, and some of these brought in additional drugs and alcohol. Faculty, more or less aware of what was going on, were demoralized. So were the students, a minority of them, who chose not to drink or smoke pot and who, some of them, had been enthusiastically looking forward to the retreat.

When they returned some of the students let on that the retreat had been a bust. Pressed for details, they gave them. Parental indignation was quickly conveyed to the school administration (I was, if memory serves, sharing tea that day with some of the masters at Eton College). The juniors were confronted en masse. For weeks, nearly every waking minute of the school director's time was spent interrogating students individually or in small groups, then afterwards conferring with chagrined, frightened, and furious parents. In the wake of this highly disruptive process, it transpired that a large percentage of the retreat participants were suspended from school for using alcohol or marijuana at a school-related event. Boys who provided alcohol or pot were dismissed. The school's investigation had inadvertently turned up the fact that three of the boys dismissed, popular and influential in their class, had been dealing drugs seriously and profitably all year. Since the initial incident in the parking lot nearly a decade earlier, there had never been a drug-related mess—or any sort of mess—of this magnitude. And the theme of the retreat had been "trust."

When the disciplinary proceedings were at last over, the headmaster wrote a letter to the parent body of the whole school, kindergarten through grade twelve, summarizing the by then much talked-about incident. The letter glossed over nothing, reiterated the school's stand against drink and drug use at school and school-related events, and concluded with a plea for parent help. He also included, perhaps to suggest we were at least thinking hard about the problem, a copy of the complete text of my manuscript, "Some Unsettling Thoughts About Settling In With Pot."[15] Two of the

---

[15] And thus began the unusual publishing history of this essay. Some of the parents were physicians who in turn sent copies of the typescript to other physicians, in Cleveland and beyond. Such was the dearth of cautionary drug literature then

secretaries at school still remember bitterly the extra labor they expended at the copying machine: 21,600 pages' worth. We began to be known, not quite deservingly, as a school "doing something" about the drug problem. And to our credit, I believe, we responded by actually beginning to do so.

that the response was outsized. The then fledgling organization, PRIDE (Parent Resources in Drug Education) in Atlanta had seen a copy and called for permission to circulate it further, which they proceeded to do in the tens of thousands. An NBC documentary producer saw the typescript, and his team came to Cleveland to talk to me and selected students about it; the documentary, when it appeared, was "Reading, Writing, and Reefer." *Thousands* of requests came into the school through the mails and over the phones, so that our very occasional University School Press produced a bound monograph thousands of copies of which were distributed at cost. A shortened version was printed in *Independent School* magazine, from which it was reprinted in *Education Digest* and over a dozen other magazines. A national feature service picked it up, divided it into a three-part series and sold it to hundreds of newspapers across the United States. A continuing stream of letters and desperate questions followed from parents, teachers, physicians, users—not *one* from a crank. There was apparently not, in 1978, much to read on the critical side of the "drug problem."

4.

RESPONDING TO STUDENT DRUG USE: ANSWERING BACK

When I returned to school in the fall after my leave of absence, it seemed the right moment for me personally and, I thought, for the school to confront student drug use through measures beyond individual "counseling" and traditional discipline. In the aftermath of the "trust" retreat, the mood of the (now) senior class was more ornery and resentful than it was chastened. There were two reasons for this. One is that the number of students disciplined the previous spring had been sufficiently large that negative peer response was negligible; if anything, the students involved cultivated a collective sense of martyrdom. There was a residue of bad feeling about the punishments given and considerable ill will directed to the students whose admissions had revealed the scope of the retreat's illicit activities, but there was not much bad feeling about drug use. Another reason for the shared sense of injury on the part of our seniors was that the students of one of the other schools involved had "stonewalled it," to use an expression from the Watergate era, in the face of their administration's investigation of the retreat; those girls therefore, in the eyes of their suspended, grounded, and, in a few instances, expelled counterparts from our school, had gotten away with it. So addressing drug issues with a student body led by this particular senior class posed a somewhat special challenge.

I. ACADEMIC RIGOR

Working to reverse a firmly entrenched cultural movement already more than a decade underway did not appear easy then, nor does it now. Even the pathways to action—where to start—did not present themselves in an obvious fashion. Looking back, it is now clear that one of the school's greatest assets in confronting drug use was something it had done all along: the school had, in the main, upheld and even increased rigorous scholastic standards. While we certainly felt the "sixties" pressures to add elective courses, while dropping required ones, to offer classes rich in "experience" (vaguely defined) as opposed to those restricted to "rote learning" (narrowly defined), and generally to lighten required standards of competency, the school's educational program steered clear of the worst excesses and insisted on high quality work. Students were and are taken through a rigorous sequence of "core courses" in western civilization, English, math, sciences, arts, languages, and physical education before, typically in their senior year, they begin to concentrate in academic areas of special interest. Advanced courses are sophisticated; "core" courses are rigorous. The typical daily homework load is from two to three hours. There has not been substantial "grade inflation"; the all-school average has ranged from the mid-to high seventies ('C' to 'C+') since I began teaching fourteen years ago. Students are promoted in grade only when they meet the course requirements of that grade. No matter what a student's special strengths and weaknesses, each takes a minimum of four years of English, three years of social studies (a prescribed sequence in Western and American Civilization), three years of foreign language, three years of mathematics (nearly all students take four), two year-long laboratory sciences (most students take three or four), two full years of arts, and four years of physical education.

What, one might ask, does this alleged rigor have to do with "the drug problem"? Scholastic rigor bears on the drug use in a very crucial way: rigorous personal demands in the classroom, in musical and athletic activities, and on the job are incompatible with drug use. If schools do not move students to the forward edge of their individual capacities to perform, many drug-related losses will not be noticed, especially early losses. Individual teachers and whole schools that have for whatever stated reasons stopped demanding rigor and concrete achievement from their students have accommodated the youthful drug epidemic. A challenging scholastic program will not by itself diminish the incidence of drug use in a school, but such a program will help to show up drug use for what it is. Because drug-using students had been failing in greater numbers and in new, distinctive patterns to meet school expectations, we were at least able to recognize a problem.

II. EDUCATING FACULTY AND STAFF

Showing a concerned faculty the effects of certain common drugs on the learning and maturation of adolescents seemed to me the most promising starting point. As I have stressed already, no one's resolve to take on the inherently unpleasant business of checking illicit drug use is likely to be stiffened unless one becomes personally and deeply convinced that real harm—retardation of learning, personality disorders, illness, death—follows from a child's involvement with drugs. In an academic community it is positively stimulating to "teach" drug prevention and remediation. I ran through the fruits of my own researches with our whole faculty the fall of my return and met periodically with smaller, voluntary groups for supplementary workshops. There was no pattern—except interest—in those who showed up for the drug information sessions. All academic departments were represented. The youngest and oldest faculty attended. All of the faculty most involved in student guidance were interested. Among the faculty as a whole, but especially among a dozen or so especially interested teachers, a consensus began to form that drug use wasn't just another face of the eternal rebellion emerging adolescents present to adult authority; that it was, rather, a distinct and very destructive syndrome of its own. Once some of us understood the basic actions of drugs, especially marijuana, on the brain, we began to see drug-involved students in a new light. The implications, for instance, of marijuana's storage in fat helped explain the timing by which students seemingly "in control" over their "partying" changed and lost function. Once we were aware that the effects of drugs were biphasic—behavior acutely altered when one is high; subtly altered long afterwards—we began to be better observers and better recorders of drug-related behavior. We learned to ask students and their parents pointed questions about drug use, and in consequence the school community got used to the fact that such questions were legitimately askable. Without making a formal resolution to do so, we shifted from a largely passive approach to drug surveillance to an active one. We no longer waited for the dramatic discipline event or the collapse of a "burnout" to act. We began, to the best of our abilities, to remediate drug users where it was known, to nip "experimental use" in the bud, and to prevent experimentation by informed and thoroughgoing drug education offerings to students.

Since the fall of 1978, half a dozen faculty have undergone specialized training in drug awareness and intervention through an organization known as Community Intervention. The intensive training has shaped an awareness of the process by which experimental use of a pleasure-producing chemical becomes casual or "social use" and how this develops, in some users, into a full-fledged dependency. Beyond the actions of various drugs themselves and the dynamics of the dependency process, these faculty have learned to identify their own inclinations to defend against bad feelings by "dependent" patterns of behavior, which may or may not include alcohol or drug use. Through this (usually illuminating, sometimes surprising) self-awareness, participants are able to see how easy it is to deny a debilitating dependency in themselves and in others. They are also taught that to deny dependent behavior—by ignoring it, by covering up for it, by forgiving it, by sharing it as a secret—is to enable it. A primary thrust of all chemical dependency remediation is to cut through the denial that something is wrong and to stop enabling the problem to continue.

In time the faculty who had undergone the special training joined me in forming a Core Group, that is, a permanent committee which meets periodically to share our own concerns and observations about possible student drug involvement and to respond to similar concerns raised by other faculty members, by parents, and by students. Members of the Core Group are both willing and trained to confront students whose problem behavior suggests drug use, whether or not that is the case. In the event that a student emerges as a concern due, say, to a convergence of indicators—tardiness, observed fatigue in class, a downturn in academic performance, perhaps casual references by other students that he is "into it" or a "big party-er," a Core Group member (or two) will arrange an appointment with the student and lay out the observed and even rumored problems. In the discussion about them, no accusation of drug use need be made, although it ought always to be brought into the discussion as a possibility: i.e., "One of the things that concerns me is that these absences and missed obligations are the kind of thing we see when a boy is getting involved with drugs." And depending on the behavior displayed, it may be appropriate to ask a student about drug involvement. Typically, in my experience, students are very frank in response. Confidentiality need not be a problem, although frightened students may sometimes try to manipulate faculty into a "trust" which is actually an enabling shield for their continued chemical use. Core Group members are representatives of the school and its stated policies, and as will be discussed ahead, the rules against drug use ought to be clear and strict. Nevertheless, this need not deter frank disclosures from students, provided that the Core Group member makes clear that while the student will not be disciplined for past behavior voluntarily disclosed in a confidential conference, the student *will* be disciplined—and the discipline will be initiated by the Core Group member—if he or she detects any violation of school policy. In other words, a student should be able to tell a Core Group member, "I smoke pot on the weekends" without being subject to disciplinary or other punitive action on the spot. But the Core Group member who is privy to such information must make his unequivocal position clear to the student: that the chemical use should stop forthwith, whether through a "no-use contract" agreed upon by Core member, student, and family, or through referral to help outside the school. Core Group members should work closely with families of students known or suspected to be involved with drugs. Students often plead with school staff not to share drug-related information with their parents. In doing so, they invariably claim extreme, cruel parental repercussions. Occasionally, this may in fact be the case; in our collective experience, however, it is almost never the case. Where students are especially fearful of their parents' response to a problem, drug-related or not, Core members ought to work through acceptable ways to bear the news, but the news must be borne. A student is not likely to stop using drugs unless the principal people in the spheres in which he moves—school, peers, home—are aware of the problem and actively support his abstinence.

When a Core Group is working effectively it will both seek out and receive drug-related information from other faculty members and students. The pooling of information ought not to be merely anecdotal; Core Group members should write it down. A single observation—"Ted looks awful in morning classes, and I can count on his being absent on Mondays"—may or may not be drug related, and it may not necessarily be cause for a confrontation. But if observations like that are recorded and stored, then further concerns are more likely to cohere. Because our school is relatively small, and faculty are more likely than not to see each other in the course of a day, our Core Group collects information both in direct conversation and through standard written forms. Questions about drug use or drug effects are seldom asked; more typically, faculty are asked, "How has _____ been in class the past few days?" or "Is _____ prepared for class this term?" The important thing about both collecting and imparting information bearing on student progress is to stick to *behavior,* not judgments. If problem behavior turns out to be derived from drug use, then close observation and confrontation of the behavior will finally reveal that fact. But whether or not drugs are the cause, the behavior should be confronted. It is also less threatening and more constructive to parents when faculty reports from the school convey observable behavior, rather than speculation.

Core Group members should meet regularly, scheduling extra sessions, as needs dictate. Members should in mutual confidence share their individual observations and the substance of student interviews they have held. They should discuss "action steps," such as when and how to share a particular concern with parents, whether to seek an outside evaluation for a suspected serious problem. Core Group members should periodically remind the larger faculty at meetings of what they are doing and clarify the routing of drug-related information. We have at times taken for granted that the faculty was well acquainted with the "Core Group" concept, and, because some of them used the process devised, we thought everyone was comfortable with it. As it turned out, some faculty, perhaps absent or inattentive during earlier sessions, did not know what the Core Group was up to and came to resent it a little as a kind of semisecret star chamber working with (and probably coddling) "druggy" kids. As with parents, the more faculty involvement there is and the more open the flow of information, the better the climate will be for resolving what drug problems there are. At all costs, a distinction between Core Group faculty as "trained experts" and other faculty as "amateurs" should be avoided. Inevitably, especially interested faculty and staff may initially take on special drug education and join a Core Group, but no faculty member should be discouraged from counseling, confronting, or in any other way addressing his or her students on drug-related concerns. What a Core Group wishes to avoid is multiple confrontations going on in ignorant isolation of each other. In practice, faculty and administrative support for Core Group activity may be uneven. This is why updated, persuasive information on drugs should be continually circulated among the faculty. The better the faculty consensus that a drug-free school is desirable and possible, the more likely it is that this will come about.

One important function of the faculty Core Group is to seek treatment for students known to be in trouble. We found that this need arose almost immediately after the Core Group was formed. There was an early confrontation with a boy who was preceded in the Upper School by unsubstantiated but persistent comments from his middle school teachers that he was "into" alcohol. In the course of several intense but supportive interviews, the boy admitted to drinking in a heavy daily pattern, about which he himself was scared and depressed. Two Core Group faculty talked with him and his family at length, then decided to establish a "no-use" agreement with the boy. During the closely monitored period that followed it was agreed that the boy could contact a Core Group member at home or at school—even in the course of a class—if he was feeling uncontrollable tension about drinking. Before two weeks had passed, the boy called a Core Group member early one morning and confessed that he had been drinking that night. A formal "intervention" was arranged with some school staff, his family, and a counselor in a local treatment center for adolescent chemical dependency. In the course of the intervention, the boy's father, mother, sister, and a teacher recounted their experiences with his alcohol use, after which the counselor suggested residential treatment. The boy submitted to this voluntarily, and after five weeks in treatment he returned to school where, supported by five more weeks of daily "aftercare" meetings, several evening AA meetings each week and an in-school "support group," he has remained sober and productive since. He did lose academic momentum, and had to repeat a course he certainly would have otherwise passed, but, with Core Group assistance, he was able to complete an honorable first year program and to win promotion into the tenth grade.

Within a few weeks of the first boy's referral, a second boy, a junior, surfaced as a problem. In this case, the concern was expressed by classroom teachers who noted heightened irritability, poor schoolwork, missed commitments, and a sloppiness in dress and grooming which they had not seen before. A standard question asked by those who had not seen him since the summer recess was, "What's happened to _____?" Student rumor and comment suggested that "_____ 'was out of control'." Direct confrontation with the boy at school was countered with energetic denials of any drug involvement. Confrontation at home—where there had been repeated instances of the boy's being intoxicated, of having drugs in his possession, of consorting with boys known to be chronic drug users—resulted in an emotional explosion. We told the boy that from our perspective he looked as if he had a problem, whether he saw it or not. Although he denied using drugs he was told that any detected instance of his doing so would result in his immediate dismissal from school; in addition, he was told that if he missed any more school commitments, we would insist that he get a formal outside "assessment" of his drug involvement. The morning after these terms were laid down, he missed a commitment—an appointment with me. When I phoned his house to find out where he was, I found that he had raised havoc there and had stormed out. The next day his parents arranged to have him admitted to treatment. The boy had told them previously that he would never go into treatment, that he would run away first. At this breakdown point at home and at school, his parents arranged to have local police officers come to their house the next day and take him to the treatment center. As with the younger boy discussed previously, there was a formal "intervention" in the treatment center. Here again, the boy was made to listen, but not allowed to respond to the effects of his drug involvements on his parents, his sisters, and on those who saw him at school. Eight days later, after a series of tests and group meetings with other student drug users, he met again with his family and me to recite his "drug history" and to declare himself chemically dependent. This admission was followed by his voluntary submission to a month of further treatment, after which he was allowed to return to school. A bright boy and previously a good student, he managed to salvage his junior year academically, although he had to drop his chemistry course and received a poorish grade in math. He too went through six weeks of "aftercare" meetings at the treatment center, attended several AA meetings per week, and was a member of an in-school support group.

    The school's support group was formed in response to a specific need, not as part of any plan or program. As it happened, a boy who had been withdrawn from the school by his parents and who had subsequently gone through drug treatment in Baton Rouge applied for readmission, and we accepted him. "But," his mother added, "he could really use a support group." We did not at the time have one, nor did we know anything about them. Our school psychologist, however, who was also a member of our Core Group, was familiar with the facilitation of other kinds of groups, and so it was decided that she and another trained Core Group member would run a support group. The initial problem was enlisting members beyond the one boy returning from Baton Rouge. The two boys mentioned above had not yet surfaced as problems, nor had they gone through treatment, although later they would join the support group. At first we reviewed our own student ranks, but concluded that, except for one boy who had been through treatment, our most likely candidates had been recently dismissed from the school. That one boy was happy to join the fledgling group. Another boy had been named by his summer camp counselor as a serious "pot problem," and a confrontation with him elicited both an agreement to refrain from all illicit chemicals and an interest in joining the group to maintain his resolve. So with three "clients" and two faculty moderators, a kernel of a group began meeting weekly, sometimes an hour before school, sometimes after school.

The premise for the support group meetings was simple, and it generated nearly all of the group's business: to discuss openly the experiences of each member as he struggled to stay drug free. It was agreed from the outset that anything brought up would be respected as confidential. Literally anything could be said, although there was a general guideline forbidding "killer statements"—put-downs and unhelpful negative judgments. In a typical meeting, members would be asked if anyone had something pressing on his mind. After these issues were aired and discussed, discussion would usually turn on how the boys were handling school, family, and social pressures. At the approach of major social events—big dances, popular concerts—the Core Group facilitators would sometimes review with members their plans for staying sober, often to the point of having them rehearse their responses to invitations which might lead to trouble. Without any question, after a session or two it was clear that the support group was a success. Members worked hard in the sessions, and they came to rely on it.

The group also grew. Although its meetings were never announced in the same way as those of activities or clubs, the group's purpose and process were written up, favorably and supportively, ly, in both the student newspaper and in a parents' newsletter. A student who attended a school nearby and who had been through treatment was comfortably accommodated. Several students tried a session or two, and some of them became permanent members. By the end of the fall term it was clear that there would be two distinct kinds of participants: those who had been through treatment and those who hadn't but wanted group support in staying straight. Early on, the group arrived at a consensus that current users would not be welcome; the strain on the others trying to remain sober was felt to be too great.

Most tellingly, the members of the group remained sober. (One boy, who had not been through treatment, had a single lapse at a party midyear, which he disclosed to a Core Group member on a Monday morning and brought before the support group. He continued to meet with the group, and there were no subsequent lapses.) Our results are either impressive or lucky, in light of the high percentage of relapses reported from treatment centers and from school support groups across the country. Two of the members of our group the first year were seniors who graduated with especially productive senior years and satisfying college acceptances. Both felt that, without the support group, they would not have endured the year, much less thrived.

But while heartened by its obvious success, we made some mistakes in setting up our support group that other schools might well avoid. Although students in the group had made presentations before the student body, before some individual classes, and before a large meeting of parents, the faculty as a whole was not clear about what the group was and what it did. A few group sessions held in the course of the school day ran long, and some faculty resented those students entering their classes late. But by far our biggest blunder was allowing students to smoke in the sessions. The question came up at once, before even the first meeting was held, as the boys who had been through treatment had been allowed to use tobacco all through the process and at all aftercare and AA meetings. Smoking had become firmly linked with therapeutic work, and our incipient support group members depended on it heavily. They had in consequence all become heavy smokers, with the reluctant blessing of their parents. The bind I felt as a decision maker (having since become Director of the Upper School) was whether to allow an obvious anomaly in our student rules—smoking is strictly forbidden our boys at school and at school events—in the interest of facilitating a small number of boys in their efforts to stay clear of more harmful drugs. The boys themselves could not have been more courteous in making the request. In the interest of getting the support group off the ground, and on the advice of the other Core Group members, I allowed the support group to smoke cigarettes. With hindsight, I see that I should not have allowed it. Moreover, I should not have made the decision without a broader student and faculty consensus. For inevitably students, some of whom were dropped from teams and otherwise disciplined for smoking cigarettes in the course of the year, pointed to the support group as privileged exceptions. Several faculty agreed. More than once, the comment was made, "The way to get what you want around here is to have a 'drug problem'." And while this was far from the case—none of the student complainers would have seriously considered the rigors undergone by the support group members—the bad feeling was real enough to become a factor in the tone of school life. The issue came to a head when three of the support group members were spotted in a car in the student parking lot at an odd hour and, when asked about it, admitted smoking. In the discipline that followed, they told the Student Discipline Committee, "Well, we're allowed to smoke in 'group,' and we just didn't think." That did it. Many of the students and some of the faculty didn't know there was smoking in the support group. Arguments were waged on both sides of this "double standard."

In hindsight, again, there should have been no arguments, because there should have been no double standard. Smoking should not have been allowed anywhere for any purpose in the school building. Our motives for allowing it were plausible, but the fact of the matter is that school communities don't do well with "double standards." Although individually capable of great subtlety in argument and thought, adolescents *en bloc* are very concrete thinkers. They respond best to clear messages, and ours, with respect to smoking, had become muddy: "If we're supposed to be extra hard on drugs, how come we let the druggy kids use one?" Finally this sentiment, combined with some faculty feeling that the very idea of drug rehabilitation, much less "support group," was extra academic, began to take a toll. As the discipline incident showed, neither the support group members nor the rest of the school was doing well with the "double standard." Before the year was out, smoking was prohibited in the support group, and Core

Group faculty renewed efforts to get smokers to quit altogether. The message, so far as we can see, is clear: it is best not to except anybody from the consequences of community rules. And the more widely known the disciplinary and remedial measures related to drug use the better.

III. REVISING SCHOOL RULES

In fact, school rules may in the long haul do as much to reduce the level of student drug use as do the most elaborate prevention and remediation programs—though one need not exclude the other. After our period of jarring disciplinary troubles through the middle seventies, I was able to convince the faculty to accept (unanimously) a change in the school's slated disciplinary policy on drug use. The change, which looks on the surface to be a very minor one, has actually had a significant impact. The previous statement on student drug and alcohol use concluded:

Students who use, exchange, or are under the influence of drugs at school or school-related events are subject to the most serious school action, including dismissal.

This statement was amended to read:

Students who use, exchange, or are under the influence of drugs at school or school-related events will be dismissed.

It is instructive that this revised, "tougher" policy was first suggested by students—and in a year when administration-student division on school policies was aggravated by residual bad feeling about the "trust" retreat. A number of students stated, in effect, that "If drugs are so harmful, why not make it cut-and-dried and expel people right away if they're caught with them? That would clear the air." Student feeling then—and I believe it was sound—was that the existing policy promised a vague sort of "trouble" if someone were caught. A "bad" consequence, but not the "worst," would befall a first offender: a short suspension, a probationary status, a detail of work, supplemented by any variety of home measures. In effect students realized the old policy amounted to a "second chance" system. In such a climate of consequences, we were told, students have a harder time saying no to drugs, as it is easier to risk "some trouble" than to risk certain dismissal.

The change, as it turns out, has been an important one for us, but at first it proved to be easier to state than to enforce. I recall clearly discussing the issue one evening at a parents' meeting, before we had changed the policy. The parents were adamant that the change should be made, that in fact it was long overdue. Like many of us at school, they had had enough. And while that sentiment would ultimately prevail, Bob Gilkeson, consulting psychiatrist to the school, stood up, if not to challenge the parents, at least to slow them down. "Make sure you can stand by this policy," he told them, "when your own child is caught in violation—because that is certainly going to happen to some of you."

Eventually our new resolve and our new policy would be tested—not, however, until a year and a half after we made the change. The intervening quiet spell on the drink and drugs front were welcome to us. The dearth of actionable offenses may have reflected poor surveillance on our part, but it was also directly connected to the disciplinary air having been cleared. Parents and students were aware that we had taken a stand and that, in regard to drug use, we stood apart from the schools surrounding us. We were no less concerned about our students' out-of-school use of alcohol and other drugs—especially the larger "open" drinking party, which had become almost the standard weekend social event. But school life itself seemed progressively productive and reassuringly school-centered.

The first detected infraction of the revised policy occurred at a formal dance at a nearby girls' school. A tenth grade girl arrived at the dance too intoxicated to walk. Once inside she passed out and could not be revived. She was whisked off for emergency treatment and spent a frightening night with her parents in the hospital before her consciousness was restored. While this drama was taking place, her escort, who did not know if his date was going to survive, "freaked out," according to eyewitness accounts. Alternately incoherent and belligerent with chaperones and police officers who detained him, he tried at one point to run away from the police but was caught. As it turned out this boy and his date and another couple had prearranged to bring some specially high proof liquor to a pre-dance party. There all four had partaken of the liquor, "smuggled" into the house in the purse of the girl who later would become ill. The party's setting is instructive. About ten couples had been invited. Food and a champagne punch had been prepared by the hostess's mother. The champagne had been added as a "harmless grown-up" touch, which was after all "safer than some of the things kids could drink." As the couples began to arrive, the hostess excused herself and went out to dine—so as not to "interfere" with the young people.

When what actually happened had been established, it was clear that the two boys who had arranged to drink and then did drink liquor before attending the dance had violated (the revised) school rule, since we had long ago made it plain that our rules extended to activities taking place in any of the independent schools which form a small association called The Cleveland Council of Independent Schools (CCIS). So here it was: two boys had shown up under the influence of alcohol at a "school-related event," and the stated punishment was dismissal. The boys were both suspended from school while the disciplinary procedures were being carried out. Both sets of parents were devastated. "You're not going to make an example out of *my* boy!" one father half-threatened, half-pleaded. We informed the parents that although the stated policy was clear, we would carry out the disciplinary process fully and carefully. But, we advised them, if our understanding of the events was correct, dismissal from the school was likely.

The school's disciplinary process for serious discipline infractions (those for which dismissal is possible) is fairly elaborate but, in my opinion, a good one. Two disciplinary committees, one composed of students elected from each class, the other composed of the faculty deans of each class and other administrators, meet separately and make separate recommendations to the school's headmaster, who decides the final verdict. Students have an opportunity to appear before both committees and may, in difficult cases, appear several times. The "facts" of this particular case were not contested. The boys were straightforward about what they had done and were contrite about it. Neither had been a disciplinary concern prior to this "incident." One of the boys was relatively inexperienced with alcohol (and also with dating and parties), the other, the boy who got drunk, was more experienced, and we probed hard in his case for signs of a drinking or drug problem. Both boys said they knew about the rule, including the fact that violation could cause dismissal, but they said they never planned to get drunk and, well, they didn't think.

The deliberations of both the student and faculty committees were extensive. In the faculty sessions, in spite of the clarity of the rule, the usual questions were raised, "O.K., these kids blew it, but what are we doing for them by banishing them?" To which would come the inevitable reply: "What are we doing for the rest of the students, and for student bodies to come, if we don't stick to our guns on this one?" Finally the issue came down to which course of action would most likely deter this kind of event from happening again. The faculty reached a consensus: the boys should be dismissed from the school, eligible to reapply another year, if their record elsewhere warranted it. The student recommendation was to stop short of dismissal, instead suspending the boys through an approaching vacation period, during which they would be required to do a daily work detail at the school. I conveyed both recommendations to the headmaster and urged him strongly to accept the one asking for dismissal. I knew both boys involved and both knew and liked their families. But it seemed clear to me (and still does) that we had a rare chance to alter the decision-making climate of our students in a healthy way, and the benefits of this outweighed even the considerable hurt these boys and their families would feel on dismissal. The headmaster addressed me with a crooked smile. There was another wrinkle. The headmistress of the school attended by the girls involved in the incident had just telephoned him to say that they were not going to dismiss the girls (one the daughter of a trustee). Moreover, we were urged to consider, for the sake of the morale at both schools, to respond as equivalently as we, in good conscience, could. My response was that the girl's school should act according to its best lights, we to ours. At length, the headmaster didn't see it that way. He determined to stop short of dismissal—but with a hitch. In granting the "reprieve" from the dictates of the new rule, he would address the student body and write a letter to every parent connected to the school to summarize the event and to share with them his recent dilemma: wanting a tough no-second-chance policy on drink and drugs but wanting also not to spoil the careers of two nice boys. The solution, therefore, would be that these two boys, after a suspension, would be retained in the school on probationary status, but their staying on meant the end of equivocation. This exception would make the rule: from now on, dismissal was our unwavering policy for boys who broke the drink/drugs rule. The ax, as he put it, had been raised over the heads of future offenders.

Clearly we equivocated—but the stated policy was as firmly entrenched as ever, and for over a year (another good school year) we may have had our cake and eaten it too. We were spared disciplinary crises involving drink and drugs, with the exception of an underclassman found to be attempting to sell drugs to other students. His parents withdrew him, obviating the need for formal discipline. When the next infraction of our drink/drugs rule occurred, however, all of us involved, including me, found ourselves equivocating.

On a cold November morning at dawn, a bunch of science students assembled at the back of the school to await the arrival of a van that would take them to Canada to pick up a load of trout eggs that would be tended through the following winter in the school's student run trout hatchery. Two boys who had been dropped off by their parents climbed into the back seat of another boy's car to wait and get warm. On the floor of the back seat of the car were two full beer bottles in a six pack left in the car by a passenger from an earlier night's revels. One of the boys, regarded universally as a great clown, twisted the cap off one of the beers and asked, "Anybody for a beer?" The driver laughed and declined. The boy took a slug and passed it to the boy at his side who also took a slug, after which the bottle, still nearly full, was returned to the carton.

All of this was observed in silhouette by the parents of another student as they too sat idling and waiting for the van. Later that morning they phoned a member of the faculty they knew well and told her what they saw. She in turn phoned me. When the boys returned from Canada I questioned them at once and received frank admissions. And so it was confirmed: two students had been caught "using alcohol at a school-related event"—parked, in fact, in the headmaster's parking place.

Had this event occurred within easy remembering of the headmaster's ax-is-in-place announcement, the course of action would have been plainer and easier to follow. As it was, it was not easy at all. One of the boys involved was a senior, the other a junior. Neither had been a disciplinary concern, both were generous contributors to school life, and the junior was a brilliant scholar. "What," we asked them repeatedly, in the course of the disciplinary hearings, "were you thinking about to take a slug of beer at 5:30 a.m. while waiting, and on school property, to go on an all-day driving excursion to Canada?" The answer in each case was convincing, "I didn't think at all." The fact of the matter, as astute parents and teachers know, is that periodically adolescents don't think at all.

For those of us in a position to decide, the issue came down to whether we would dismiss these boys for an ill-considered slug of beer while, technically, "at school." More specifically, we were deciding on the status of our rule which we still felt, despite the present dilemma, was important and right. Expecting the worst, the boys and their parents were already shattered. Uncharacteristically for me, and I believe appropriately, I decided that a strict application of the rule in this case would neither send a coherent message to the student body, nor would it in any way serve the interests of the students involved. My colleagues, even the most rigid, agreed. Suspension, probation, denial of extracurricular privileges were applied but the boys were not dismissed.

This time I chose to make the speech before the student body. In it I reviewed the history of our concern about drink and drugs from when the school first began to experience their ravaging effects a decade earlier. I reviewed the sentiment that had gone into our adopting a "no second chance" policy. Then—and this was the hard part—I proceeded to explain how we, wisely or not, decided not to apply it in the previous two instances. The first infraction, I said, set the policy in gear, made it real. Had a second infraction like it occurred, the boys involved would have been dismissed. But the next infraction wasn't anything like it. It violated the letter more than the spirit of the strict policy. I told the students that, by rights, the boys involved should have been kicked out, but we were making an exception, an exception which we again hoped would make the rule. All seemed satisfied with this resolution, but those of us most involved in drug prevention activities at school were not sure.

The next violation of the rule occurred exactly a year later (after yet another good school year), and it was not difficult to decide. A boy entering a Halloween dance was observed to be "not quite right" in the opinion of a faculty chaperone, a Core Group member. On interviewing the boy, it was obvious from his breath that the boy had been drinking. While clearly affected by the alcohol ("two or three beers," he said), he was not falling down drunk. His parents were called and he was taken home. In the inquiry and disciplinary proceedings that followed it transpired that the boy had gone over to his girl friend's house to pick her up and devise a costume for the dance. No adults were home, but a live-in college student was in charge of the household. A decision was made to send out for some pizza, which they then ate. In addition the boy and the college student had "a few beers." The boy was in no doubt as to the school's policy. We had just concluded an extended three-week program for parents and students on the effects of drink and drugs on adolescent development, had in fact invited some of the nation's leading anti-drug spokesmen to address us. I had myself talked to the assembled student body before the dance, reminding them explicitly that if they showed up under the influence of alcohol or other drugs, they would be dismissed. The boy was aware of this, but, again, "wasn't thinking." The decision was to dismiss him, with an understanding that if he performed well for a term or more at another school, we would consider his readmission.

While not on balance a controversial decision, there were some student grumblings; a popular tenth grader had been removed from their midst. Some of them challenged me: "Did I think _____ was the *only* boy to have come to a dance after drinking some beers?" I told them I didn't know, but if I found out there were others, I would be glad to discipline them. The teacher who detected the boy's drinking was also challenged: "How could you ---?" The teacher's response was, how could he not, given his responsibilities as a teacher and a chaperone. He let those who asked know that he stood by the school's policy. Several of us told students that a better question was, "How could he (the student)?!!" (Which, in fairness, was asked by a number of students.)

In the winter of the same school year another boy, a senior, was dismissed from school and subsequently attended a chemical dependency treatment center in Minneapolis. In this case, the faculty Core Group had been apprised of what looked like an alcoholic drinking pattern on the part of this boy outside school. The parents, alert and cooperative from the outset, confronted the boy with his drinking at home, forbade any further use and, finally, had him evaluated by a physician trained in detecting alcoholism. The boy continued to see the physician on an outpatient basis, but word trickled out to faculty that the drinking continued. Then one afternoon a teacher smelled alcohol on the boy in the course of an exam, confronted and confirmed it, and we sent him home. We informed the parents soon after that there was no question of his returning to school without successfully completing residential treatment for chemical dependency.

The disciplinary process did not have to be set in motion, as the parents withdrew the boy and enrolled him in a treatment program. Although structurally very different from the preceding incident, this boy's withdrawal from school helped establish in the student mind (with benefits to be described) that "If you get caught with alcohol or drugs, you go."

IV. DRUG EDUCATION AND PREVENTION

While a number of our faculty were becoming increasingly well-trained to respond to drug use, and while our school disciplinary policy was, by fits and starts, taking shape, our students were also being instructed about the biological and medical effects of drug use. From the outset it has been our experience that high-content, high-energy presentations about drugs are well received by students from the primary grades up through the high school. In addition to presentations I personally make to all the students in the Upper School's required health course, we also make special presentations to all new students when they enter the school. We also address whole classes (seventh through tenth grades especially) on the subject, and we periodically invite present and former students to school to share their experiences while they were in trouble with drugs.

There is a tendency on the part of both faculty and students to feel, "all right, we've done that," after a school program on drug abuse. But, like cheating, stealing, intolerance or any other traditional school problem, drug awareness is never "taken care of." Every autumn, at least one quarter of every high school is composed of new students. Moreover, the adolescent time frame is significantly different from an adult's. Single strong impressions carry over for days and even weeks, but rarely for months, still more rarely for years. Children realize that what the adult order considers important is stressed repeatedly. We talk to students about drugs in every imaginable format: in all-school assemblies, in classrooms, in all-class meetings, in informal conferences. We invite in guest "experts" frequently, but we rely more frequently on presentations by our own faculty and students. As long as alcohol and other drugs are a factor in children's decision-making, it is hard to "overdo" precautions—this at least has been our experience.

By far the most enjoyable, and I believe most fruitful, form of drug abuse prevention is teaching what drugs do to health and to personality. Older children and adolescents typically have not had much immersion in psychology, so it is interesting to construct with them a "model" of personality development corresponding to the ages of the class or audience. The object is to show some of the complexity of physical and mental development, while showing the direction of the changes taking place: from slower to faster brain wave activity, from underdeveloped to fully developed organs and capacities, from simpler to more complex mental operations. It is reassuring for adolescents to hear that the rapid changes they are undergoing are universal, and that some of the worrying reactions to these changes, including moodiness, insistent sexual urges, feelings of alienation and hostility to formerly congenial family members, are in fact common to everyone. The personal, social, familial, and scholastic stresses should also be identified as necessary conditions for maturation. The lesson is that the discharge of stressful anxiety through achievement is the very mechanism of personal development. Stress may feel unpleasant, and unmanageable levels of it may shut down the personality altogether, but it is nonetheless what drives one's personal engine to adapt and to grow.

It can be instructive to discuss with early and older adolescents typical responses to stress. The most ordinary dilemmas bear examining: telephoning a girl one does not know very well to ask for a date; finding oneself suddenly, and perhaps unexplainably, on the outside of the "in" group; failing to distinguish oneself—perhaps even being cut from a team—in a sport one loves passionately; getting low grades when all those sitting around one are receiving higher ones. The possibilities are endless. What the teacher/discussion leader should help to bring out is the adaptive defenses used to manage the stress: for example, denial that one "cares" about the loss, rejection, poor grades, etc. Students can be made to understand that it is no accident, nor a peculiar characteristic of their generation, that not caring (or seeming not to) has been the most durable adolescent pose in history. To an extent every adolescent assumes the pose, at least temporarily, but beyond a certain point, not caring begins to be destructive, especially when it leads one to stop taking risks—to stop calling the girl who might say no, to stop trying out for teams, to stop working hard for scholastic results that never seem to come anyway, etc.

Students will have no trouble recognizing the common sources of stress and the equally common defenses erected in response.

What many will not have considered, however, is how the introduction of mood-altering chemicals affects the process of stress management. Children high on pot or drunk or "tripping" on LSD, whatever else they are feeling, are not processing here-and-now reality accurately, if at all. Anxieties felt while they were sober are blurred or blocked while they are high. The developmental effects of this are really double. First, stress may be effaced by the action of the drug, which in itself is experienced pleasurably. Secondly, the loss of mental function responsible for diminished strength is rewarded by powerful waves of sensual feelings.

When they are not frightened, drug-using adolescents typically say they use drugs because it feels good—for pleasure. Just as typically, they deny using them as a result of "peer pressure" or because they want to escape a problem. Moreover, they are not lying when they make these claims. A counselor may see a clear relationship between a painful peer rejection or a wrenching divorce and the onset of a child's drug use, but the child himself will not see it that way. He does not see it because when he first experimented and succeeded in getting high his conscious routine was very likely to satisfy his curiosity, to experience a new thrill. He is unlikely to consider, especially at the outset of his use, that the residual bad feelings he had been experiencing were effaced while he was high. And while he does not see it, he has begun to manage those bad feelings with a chemical. Moreover, because the feelings were so pleasurably "managed" while he was high, they were not managed by any other more productive means. In this sure way, drug taking comes to replace healthy stress management. For without any question, the most frustrating aspect of working with drug-altered young people is their inability to attach feelings to dramatic events, such as school failures, legal scrapes, family disintegration, etc. When they are detoxified in treatment and are able to consider these things soberly, they feel terrible. Their defenses against such feelings are usually underdeveloped, since their development ceased with the commencement of their drug use.

When drug use first became an unavoidable issue in schools over a decade ago, some school administrations and parent groups decided that it would be informative to hear from "the kids" themselves on drugs—current and former users. "These kids know what's happening on the street. They'll tell it like it is." This approach was not, and is not, fruitful for two reasons. The first is that "street knowledge" doesn't include much that is substantial, and it usually includes a great deal that is untrue. A child or a teenager who uses drugs "knows" the physical appearance of the substance he or she takes, knows the price, the nickname (i.e., "black beauties," "ludes," "Thai sticks," "acid," etc.) and the interior sensations he or she experiences. All this can sound very knowing, but none of it bears at all on what one needs most to know: the actual effects of the substances on health and personality. Drug dealers, especially those who deal to children, are not known for being fastidious about what they actually put into capsule, bag, powder, or tab. The other reason testimony from "the kids on the street" is misleading is that it supports a kind of "counter-culture" response in young users: an I-could-tell-you-stories-that-would-make-your-hair-curl posture that simultaneously diminishes the hearer's confidence in controlling and understanding the "drug scene" while reinforcing the status of drug users by deferring to their "expertise." Active drug users are notoriously blind to the effects of their drug use, since the capacity to perceive the effects is altered by the drugs.

Students should be instructed as to the basic actions of the most available drugs in each major group: depressants (opiates, alcohol, etc.), stimulants (cocaine, amphetamine, etc.), and hallucinogens (LSD, marijuana, mushrooms, etc.). But, as indicated earlier, it should be stressed that different classes of chemicals can be experienced in a similar way by users, just as the same substance can affect different users differently. That is, a depressant like alcohol can knock out inhibitions, so that the user feels "up" or belligerent, while in another user it knocks out active functions, so the user feels deadened and sleepy. "Speed" is usually taken to activate neural capacity, so that the user feels a hyper-alertness, but stimulants can also activate suppression (which is why some stimulant-like drugs are used as medicine for hyper-activity and certain learning disabilities), which diminishes perception and other capacities. The point underlying all of this descriptive information, of course, is to help students see that mind-altering chemicals are taken for the pleasurable effects they produce. Part of the pleasure, however, is the distortion and loss of healthy functions. And once again, losses which (1) are accompanied by sensual ecstasy and feelings of elation which require little effort and no skill to reproduce, (2) delay or replace anxieties, and (3) are not perceived as losses may well be risks children are willing to take. They will be less willing, however, if they understand the appeal and the dynamics of drug use prior to trying drugs themselves.

Healthy, productive students often have a hard time relating personally to recovering drug users when they make presentations at school—although such presentations are valuable in other ways. It is easy, even for beginning users, to write off the person who has "been there" as a hard case, someone whose personal idiosyncracies, not drugs, caused the problem. In a way, the tales of chronic abuse, physical misery, and nightmare confrontations with family, school, also can serve to reassure a "casual" user that "I'm not like that—that's nothing like our scene." Students are apt to understand that "hard case" better and to regard early drug use more critically if they are taught that chemical dependency is often a deceptively gradual process, the stages of which flow predictably into one another. A very productive class period or two (or lecture or two) might be given over to a presentation and discussion of the Stages of Dependency, a common model used by many chemical dependency treatment centers across the country. Although worded differently in different manuscripts and in different regions of the country, the stage theory maintains that the initial phase of drug use involves successfully getting high for the first time, feeling sufficient pleasure and a sufficient lack of negative consequences to want to repeat the experience. At this point, the user has learned the mood shift. When subsequent highs have occurred to the extent that one begins to base planned activity and personal relationships upon drug using, the user, whether he is fully conscious of it or not, has passed into the stage of seeking the mood shift. As drug use becomes regular, the substances used are no longer able to produce a sharp increment of pleasure over the "normal" state. Because of the various ways psychoactive drugs deplete the healthy nervous system, the user comes to feel unendurably bad both physically and emotionally unless he or she takes a drug. At this point the user is becoming intoxicated to feel "normal"; all behavior is now organized around maintaining the mood shift. Students hearing this presentation should be made aware of the relationship between their own "stage" (non-user, early user, etc.) to the stage just ahead of it. The student who cannot imagine progressing to the chronic condition described by the "hard case" may easily imagine progression into the plausible "next step" of "experimentation" or "occasional" use. Recovering users speaking to student audiences should be asked to dwell on their early use, their use up to the point they feel they lost control over it. Students in my experience have less trouble "relating" to that.

In the course of drug education presentations and discussions, students raise challenging questions, and it is very important that they get good answers. Certain of these questions have become almost standard. "Despite the dangers associated with them," somebody will ask, "don't some drugs expand the mind?" Here students should be reminded of what drugs do to incoming sensory information: they distort it, substitute (by "incorrectly" retrieving) other sensory data for it, or they block it altogether. The resulting experience may be interesting—stupefyingly so—and it may be accompanied by powerful sensual feelings, but it is a distortion of healthy function, experienced at the cost of possible damage to the nervous system sites affected. Students who claim they "never really heard" some kind of music or "never really saw" some common visual object until they were high should be told that, yet, they did hear and see those things before, but it was not complex enough to activate their interest. The mind "contracted" to a condition of wonder at the commonplace, commonplace at least for those past infancy.

"How come," somebody will ask, "Ted can smoke pot regularly and still be a lot better student than I am, when I don't use any drugs at all?" This is an important question, because most teenagers can point to somebody who is "into drugs" and apparently managing well—possibly even having an extra good time. Students—and adults too—should evaluate the effects of drug use on a user's own potential performance, not just against general norms. It has been our experience that the drug use of very bright students is harder to detect than that of weak ones, because abler students can lose considerable function (especially the synthesis of new information) and still get by in school programs, especially if the upper limit of their intelligence isn't being challenged. In teaching, we must occasionally remind ourselves that we often do not know the upper range of students who give us all we require (and perhaps more) on examinations, papers, and projects. When a student of mine receives an A, that is an indication that he has thoroughly met my expectations, not, necessarily, that he has reached his full potential. For a time, a bright student using drugs may still get A's and B's; this is especially likely if he is only required to retrieve previously stored information from previously formed mental structures. Another factor masking actual performance deficits in drug-using students is the natural tendency of teachers (despite our protests that we don't do it) to pigeon-hole students into a grade range. This is more likely to happen in arts, English, history, and social studies courses than it is in math, languages, and science, where the instruments to measure progress are usually more objective. Students wondering honestly "how Ted gets by using drugs" should be encouraged to look at how Ted is doing compared to how he has done in the past and how he could do at his best. Is he doing more or less work since he began using drugs? Is he more heavily committed to activities or less so? Does he look *ahead*? Make good plans? Does he initiate much in the way of new activity and learning?

"Tell me something," the drug education expert is asked. "Have you *tried* it?" In some settings this question is amusing, in others dramatic. There is no reason to be afraid of it. The answer—besides "yes" or "no"—is that the question is beside the point. More specifically, it is based on the erroneous assumption that the experience of taking a drug will better prepare one to evaluate its harmful effects. As stated already, one of the specific effects of mind-altering drugs is that they interfere with the very capacity to evaluate. Trying drugs to evaluate consequences (although undertaken seriously by early drug researchers, lacking other data) is rather like taking a potion that makes one forget and then trying to remember what it was like. The "have you tried it?" challenge is appropriately directed only at those who claim drugs produce no pleasure. But drug educators do not dispute that drugs produce pleasure; they have an educated fear of what chemically induced pleasures can do to personality. The drug educator attempts to demonstrate the connection between drug use and learning losses, health problems, personality changes, and a variety of related harms. The validity of these data is not in the least affected by whether the person presenting it has tried a drug.

Without fail, someone will ask, "What about legalization?" This can be exasperating to deal with, especially after one has already outlined the personal and social hazards which have kept most psychoactive drugs at least technically illegal. But the question is instructive for what it shows about how students use "legitimacy" to decide value questions. For concrete thinkers of all ages, the "law" may well be the supreme moral category: when a proposition has been demonstrated to be within the law, it is acceptable; against the law, unacceptable. This extreme legalism is especially common through mid-adolescence. Nevertheless, it is important to answer the question by pointing out to students that, at least in parliamentary systems, the law is the result of legislator's considering the same kinds of information and issues the students have just been considering. The primary aim therefore is to reach a consensus about what drugs do; only when such a consensus is reached can lawmakers begin to deliberate wisely. Students are usually aware, for instance, that some jurisdictions have "decriminalized" the possession of small amounts of marijuana. This will, for the concrete legalist, make marijuana use acceptable. The same individual will also find marijuana use unacceptable in jurisdictions where it is illegal. Obvious as it may sound, the job of the teacher is to point out that the effects of marijuana on users will not vary with strict or lenient laws. A law is a social answer to a problem. Harmless phenomena require no laws to restrict them; harmful phenomena do.

V. ORGANIZING PARENTS

All the responses discussed so far in this chapter—the efforts of informed faculty, the shift in disciplinary policy, the drug education presentations—have come together to clear the air with respect to student drug use. This is not to say that students never challenge the school's stand or that a student will never again go astray. But students are clear about the school's position. Moreover, school life is substantially drug free. Outside of school, however, students have continued to move in a social setting in which drugs of all kinds are easily available and in which drinking is considered a norm at large gatherings, whether supervised by adults or not. By no means does the parent body as a whole accept underage drinking as a norm (though some do), but until a few years ago, most felt powerless to alter their children's "party scene." Perhaps in response to the school's presentations and other drug-related communications sent from school, perhaps because some of them had been moved to action by family crises, our parents began to organize themselves to address student drug use in the fall of 1982. The catalyst seems to have been a school-wide parent forum put together by a planning committee of parents and school staff over the summer. The program would consist of three consecutive Wednesday evening presentations in September and was titled "A Parents Awareness Forum on Drink, Drugs, and Youth." The first two sessions consisted of presentations by nationally prominent "experts," practicing physicians who had taken up drug abuse prevention as a major public health issue. The format for the first two sessions was a pointed address by the guest speaker, followed by an hour or so of audience questions fielded by a panel composed of the speaker, local physicians and psychiatrists, and school staff. These sessions were in fact very good. My own muted fear about kicking off a school year with such a heavy emphasis on a single issue proved to be groundless. The speakers were bright and very current in their research and survey references. Moreover, both guests were unequivocal: drug use by the young, even in the seemingly "conservative" eighties, was in their professional opinion, and in their practices, a medical emergency. Both stated strongly that the social dimension of the remedy was a drug-free climate for youth. "A little beer" was no exception; in fact, it was claimed, "a little beer" had become an unprecedented epidemic of teenage drinking. That parents were not in control of the phenomenon seemed hard to deny. That they might regain control was held out as possible. The speakers struck a responsive note. Questions had to be cut short, reluctantly, long after the allotted time had run out—with a promise to answer others in a published "proceedings" of the forum. But perhaps the clearest—and most surprising—message conveyed at the evening sessions was that so many parents were experiencing, in isolation of one another, the same frustrations and fears. Again and again parents came forward to say, "I thought we were the only family in town who was concerned about kids drinking—it looks to me as if we're all in the same boat." Student protests that "everybody else gets to drink" began to be regarded more critically by many parents.

The third and final session was, if anything, more successful than the first two. The guest presenter was a young alumnus who was a recovering alcoholic and multiple drug abuser. His drinking had begun while he was an underclassman at the school, and his prominent family could be considered a stereotypical school family. In other words, he was "one of us," and on this account hard not to take seriously. Although he had spoken to our students several times at my request, he had never before addressed a parent group (which included his own parents). His story was harrowing. The first drinking experiences were trivial, childish; mischievously draining glasses after a family party. Then he described two full years of drinking and drug taking in a spirit of mischievous acting out, a period in which he felt completely in control of what he was doing. This experience evolved into a pattern of drinking in order not to feel bad. From this time forward, until he stopped drinking and using drugs four and a half years later, he recounted an unbroken succession of family confrontations, lies, thefts, hospitalizations, lost days, and nearly fatal illness until extended hospital treatment combined with AA membership to begin his recovery. Following his talk, he joined a panel of current students, two of whom had been through chemical dependency treatment themselves and two others, both student leaders, who agreed to represent "typical students." The first question asked was, "How much drinking is there now? Are there more drinking parties or more non-drinking parties?" The answers from all five panelists surprised the parents. Alcohol was either served or brought in at every party the boys had attended since they were in the middle school.

The parent response to the "Awareness" program was deeply concerned but also very positive. Dozens of participants, some with a "problem" in the family but most not, volunteered to organize follow-up activity, perhaps even on a permanent basis. The result of their efforts is an increasingly active Parents Awareness Network. After the September forum, a letter was sent to the whole parent body summarizing what was said (the complete "Proceedings" was sent that winter) and inviting parents to join a schoolwide Network. By "joining" (checking a box on a return slip and supplying signatures and phone numbers) parents agreed to supervise social gatherings held in their homes, not to serve alcohol or any other illegal substance to children under age, to inform other parents of drink or drug involvement on the part of their children, when there is first-hand knowledge of the involvement, and to be willing to have similar information conveyed to them by other parents.

A large majority of the parents expressed interest. Nearly all the parents of students through grade ten signed on, with decidedly more modest returns from eleventh and twelfth grade. Several parents wanted clarification of the Network's "terms" and others wanted to augment them. So another evening meeting was called for clarification and open discussion. This meeting was a critical one, as the parents divided into groups according to their sons' school grade. Parents therefore were able to talk about "party" concerns, curfews, and inoffensive ways to communicate concerns to families of their sons' actual friends. Again, confidence was boosted, confidence that parents could help shape the out-of-school, out-of-household experiences of their children.

The biggest obstacle raised to enthusiastic participation in the network idea came from parents who said they had a hard time imagining picking up the telephone to inform somebody, perhaps unknown to the caller, that their child had been observed stoned or drunk. They agreed it should be done—they certainly would want to know as much about their own children—but they simply doubted they would do it in the event. Other parents balked at the same provision, worried that the repercussions would be hard on their children at school afterward. In checking with parents connected to similar networks elsewhere, the same reluctance was reported. A compromise was proposed and accepted according to which parents who preferred not to contact the family of the youngster about whom there was an alcohol or drug-related concern could contact the school's faculty Core Group instead. The Core Group could then, at its discretion, pass the information on to the family involved, with the understanding that if the reported incident indicated a pattern of drug use or drinking, it would definitely be brought to the family's attention. To date, this policy seems to be serving well; a number of parents have made direct contacts to other Network families, while several others have been in touch with our Core Group faculty.

Our tentative Network actually began to function when the names of participants were organized into a "directory" and mailed to all the school's parents. The nature of Network contacts has varied. Parents are now more apt to phone the parent hosts of parties to which their children are invited to be sure of the party's hours, that there will be adult supervision, and that alcohol is not being served. When an unsupervised party is discovered—typically when a student's parents are out of town—parents of the host, when they return, are informed. The parents of one of our boys recently returned home from a business trip early and found evidence of a drinking party at their house, strictly forbidden in their household's policy. They proceeded to write the families of all their son's friends indicating what had happened, how disappointed they were at their own boy's breach of trust, and what his punishment was going to be. The letter concluded with a note to the boys, "If you were there, I hope all of this makes you think, because you have really let us down." In every instance the parents contacted were grateful.

Since the initial appeal for a Network, our parents have generated a running stream of meetings, most of them at the class or friendship group level. And whereas the initial emphasis was on clarifying terms of Network membership and setting up supplemental "expert" presentations, the current interest is knowing other parents better and establishing more comfortable contacts. As a result parents who have been through or who are going through a "drug problem" in the family no longer feel alienated and unsupported. Even more typically, parents (nearly all of them) who felt they were anachronistically holding the anti-drinking and drugs fort alone have discovered allies. A less grim and a more lighthearted mood prevails at home and school meetings.

Predictably, there has been a student response to the formation of a parent network, especially as school and families have been increasingly drawn together. Our more socially precocious students were most uneasy, especially while the Network was defining itself. But this is easily endured. More than anything else, our students want to know if their parents mean it. Some have challenged their parents: "What's the matter, don't you trust us?" The answer (at its best) has been, "We trust you as much as ever, but we don't trust what happens when teenagers illegally drink and use drugs. Whatever we can do to prevent that, we will." A surprising number of students I have talked to are grateful for the extra controls. Others don't really mind, so long as their friends are similarly treated. When students gripe to me about their parents' zealous surveillance, I always ask, "What do you think they are most afraid of?" The question invariably leads to good discussion. So our parents are now actively and self-consciously responding to youthful drug use. They seem as a body much more willing than at any other time I can remember to contact each other to ask questions or to register opinions. There is an emergent mood among them that they have a right to know where their children are and to have a reasonably clear idea of what they are doing. Several have "risked" and been gratified by the success of "alternative" (drink and drug free) parties and recreation. One small delegation has effectively bawled out some merchants well known to sell beer to teenagers. In another community a group of our Network parents has brought pressure to bear to shut down a notorious "head shop." Liberal and conservative, black, white, and oriental, well-to-do and low-income parents seem to be able to come together effectively on the drug-prevention issue.

5.

BRIGHT SIGNS

In the earlier chapters of this section, I tried to suggest what it was like for my colleagues and me to have experienced the impact of the past decade's student drug epidemic. What happened to students who got in trouble, what their families went through, what we went through with their families, and the less tangible but still inescapable effect the "drug problem" had on the tone of school life—these things would be hard to exaggerate. Without question, it is stressful and demoralizing to work in a school where drug use has taken hold. Moreover, it may seem, and actually be, extra stressful to challenge drug use. But when the challenge begins to have an effect, the rewards are boundless.

There is little in my own professional experience that has been more gratifying than seeing a student emerge productive and drug free after a sustained period of chemical dependency. Since our guidance staff has become trained in drug abuse prevention, we are now able to exchange information openly and frankly with parents, both parties no longer wondering darkly, but never mentioning, what part "drugs" might play in the child's problem behavior.

As we have become clearer in our prohibition of alcohol and drug use, it has progressively diminished as a factor in school life. In consequence the tone of school life has changed markedly. Students have less resistance to being passionately invested in projects, activities, and sports. We have over the past three years experienced an energizing resurgence of athletic excellence, of sophisticated science research projects, of superior dramatic performances and literary achievements. By showing a willingness to confront and to work with suspected drug users, we have shown that we are not "out to get" them—just their drug use. Many of the individuals so confronted have been appreciative and even affectionate on that account—none more so than those who have returned from treatment and have been supported in their sobriety both by faculty and fellow students.

It is a positive pleasure also to teach responsive students about the effects of drugs on maturation and health. Needing to have the answers to the good questions students invariably raise drives us on to find them, to learn. My own colleagues, and the drug education experts elsewhere I have had a chance to meet in the course of drug-related work over the past decade, are all in agreement that the greatest benefit of studying the effects of "drugs" is the respect and knowledge gained of the functions drugs impair. Thus in trying to understand "drugs," we find ourselves emerging with a more complete understanding of the developmental psychology of adolescence, of learning, and of thinking itself.

And as I have said, school life feels better. This past spring, our seniors, although all safely admitted to colleges and well into what in past years has been the heart of their "senior slump," managed to get really excited about their prom. A band leader of considerable celebrity was somehow talked into bringing his orchestra to Cleveland, and there was much advance talk of a "prom to end all proms." Prodigious amounts of money were charmed out of those who had it. Decorations were elegant. The police chief of our jurisdiction was lulled into agreeing to a midnight display of fireworks on the school's grounds. The parents themselves were rather aching to attend this dance, and fourteen sets of them did. Moreover, it all came off. For the first time in faculty memory most students showed up to the prom as it began and, once inside, proceeded to dance, mix, and generally spread themselves around with an ease of manner and verve which confirmed that something new was afoot in student life. As has been our routine for several years now before dances, we made several warnings about showing up at the dance "under the influence," but this time it almost seemed that the warnings might have been superfluous. The faculty and parent chaperones, the headmaster, and the students agreed that there was not a sign of alcohol at the dance. This was confirmed the next day by the school's maintenance staff whose job had been, in past years, clearing up the beer cans and liquor bottles left in the student parking lot. And for the juniors who attended the dance, this was how a prom should be: a model for their own. And so, one hopes, it goes in school life.

Before closing, I would like to clarify what may be an important point. I have made enough references to individual students who have been in trouble with alcohol and other drugs and enough references to the toll this took on the quality of school life to suggest that we have indeed had "a drug problem." If so, fine; we did. And on that account our example may be useful to others. But it also occurs to me that a reader might, on the basis of these disclosures, write us off as an especially "druggy" school, perhaps one whose problems were of our own, or of our region's, making. For many reasons this would be a mistake. Even during our most embattled "sixties," even during the period of our least effective response to student drug use (our intensive "counseling" period), our school has been selected by parents for the greater likelihood that drugs would not come to bear on student life. To put it more bluntly, at our worst we have been regarded as a haven from "the drug problem." At our best, we are such a haven—although other schools in the region are mobilizing against drugs, too. Bringing school drug problems to light does raise flack in the community, but it is the job of educated people to connect those bad feelings to drugs, not to the school or to the individuals who have the problem. This can be done. Drug use can be challenged and reversed. At the time of writing, the toughest argument against drug use at our school is more likely to come from a student than from a teacher. And with every increment of progress, school life brightens, and the school's regard in the community is enhanced.

On the brink of commencement last year, a senior wandered into my office. It was a boy I knew well and liked very much, although I had been concerned about him and some of his friends for several years. He is a bright, well-informed boy who had been active in school service projects and who at times flirted with being a good scholar. Although I didn't teach him, we used to have occasional long talks after school, more than once lasting through what should have been the dinner hour. The reason I was concerned about him is that the "word" on his group was that outside of school they were "heavy social drinkers." I had confronted him about the rumors several times—in fact, nearly every time we spoke. He acknowledged some drinking. I told him he ought to be worried about it. For one thing, he was breaking faith every time he drank; specifically, he was breaking the law, was deceiving his parents (they too were aware of and concerned about his drinking), and he was breaking the spirit of the school's policy.

Beyond these breaches of faith, I told him, he ran a risk of becoming dependent on alcohol. I asked him how much he drank, in what circumstances, how often he got drunk. I asked him to consider carefully whether he had begun to plan for his drinking, to organize his time around it. He was usually fairly straightforward in reply, and I think he did some serious reflecting about his drinking, but I do not think he stopped—even after the summer of his junior year when he had a frightening auto accident while under the influence of alcohol. It was always good to see this boy and to talk to him, but there was an element of tension in our relationship that never disappeared. Whether or not I mentioned it, his drinking was always on my mind, and he was, I am sure, aware of this and somewhat uneasy about it.

One afternoon before commencement he brought up the drinking issue. He acknowledged that a lot of the drinking that went on was irresponsible, but he asked me if I didn't agree that student drinking was a reaction to the "tightening up" on the school's and now the parents' part. "Don't you think that makes kids want to drink?" he asked. I asked him if restrictions on drinking made him want to drink? He said no, but he thought defiance might be a motive for other drinkers. What he was asking me, essentially, was whether I thought our drug prevention efforts had stimulated—caused—some of the very problems we were out to solve. I told him no, and, on careful analysis, the answer really is no. I told him a little about Paul and about how, when his father put his foot down on pot, Paul continued to use it just to defy him. To an observer fresh on the scene, Paul had a "father problem." But he did not have a father problem before he had a pot problem, and he had the pot problem before he had a father problem. By the same token, I told my senior friend, students might well feel defiance and hostility about restrictions when they drink, but in fact drinking (and other drug use) was far more pervasive, at least among our students, before the restrictions. The restrictions were caused by the "drug problem." If the restrictions caused anything, they caused students to stop. I also asked him to consider carefully the extent to which the we-drink-to-show-up-excessive-restrictions position actually makes it easier to do something he and his friends feel substantially ambivalent about. Convincing themselves that their drinking, however deceptive and illicit, is an expression of a cause, makes them feel less bad about breaking rules. It also contributes to a special feeling of mutual solidarity.

My friend warmed to this point, "Exactly!" he said. "But is rebellion such a bad thing? Isn't rebellion necessary at certain times in life? Isn't it really a bad thing that there's so little rebellion around these days?" Rebellion, I told him, was neither good nor bad in itself. Rebels committed to humane and life-preserving values are usually held up as heroes in history. The value of rebellion depends not on its intensity, but on what it's about. "If you mean what you are telling me," I told him, "you are saying that your rebellious feelings terminate in drinking, in being drunk. What kind of rebellion is that?" This point he seemed to accept, admitting that he had recently argued along the same lines with a friend who was defending drinking. "You can say we drink for fun or for the hell of it," he said he told his friend, "but you can't say it does any good."

"But still," he told me thoughtfully, "it seems that we're the last class that has anybody willing to rebel."

"You mean to drink?"

"No, not just that. Last weekend a bunch of us were trying to rile up the juniors. We told them 'they're closing in on you. The school's closing in, the parent Network is closing in, and you aren't going to do anything about it.' They don't even care! They're just going to go about their business. It seems to me that a lot of stuff that got started in the Sixties is coming to an end."

What I didn't say then, because he already knew, is that I hope, in at least one restricted sense, he is right.

Booklets Available From the American Council for Drug Education

Blasinsky, M. and Russell, G. K. (Eds.) *Urine Testing for Marijuana Use: Implications for a Variety of Settings.* American Council on Marijuana, New York; $2.50.

Cohen, S. *Cocaine Today.* American Council on Marijuana, New York; $2.50.

Cohen, S. and Andrysiak, T. *Therapeutic Potential of Marijuana's Components.* American Council on Marijuana, New York; $2.50.

Cohen, S. and Lessin, P. J. *Marijuana and Alcohol.* American Council on Marijuana, New York; $2.50.

de Silva, R. and DuPont, R. L. (Eds.) *Treating the Marijuana-Dependent Person.* American Council on Marijuana, New York; $2.95.

Heath, R. G. *Marijuana and the Brain.* American Council on Marijuana, New York; $1.50.

Lantner, I. and Barth, R. *A Pediatrician's View of Marijuana,* American Council on Marijuana, New York; $2.50.

Marijuana: *The National Impact on Education.* American Council on Marijuana, New York; $2.95.

Moskowitz, H. and Petersen, R. *Marijuana and Driving.* American Council on Marijuana, New York; $2.50.

Petersen, R., Cohen, S., Jeri, F. R., Smith, D., and Dogoloff, L. *Cocaine: A Second Look.* American Council on Marijuana, New York; $2.50.

Russell, G. K. *Marijuana Today: A Compilation of Medical Findings for the Layman.* The Myrin Institute, New York; $3.00.

Smith, C. G. and Asch, R. H. *Marijuana and Reproduction.* American Council on Marijuana, New York; $2.50.

Tashkin, D. P. and Cohen, S. *Marijuana Smoking and Its Effects on the Lungs.* American Council on Marijuana, New York; $2.50.

Turner, C. E. *The Marijuana Controversy: Definition, Research Perspective and Therapeutic Claims.* American Council on Marijuana, New York; $1.99.

Free catalog on additional materials and films available upon written request.

BOARD OF DIRECTORS
Mrs. Gioia Marconi Braga
Carol Burnett
Kenneth I. Chenault, Esq.
Robert L. DuPont, M.D.
Mrs. Helen Clay Frick, II
M. G. H. Gilliam, Esq.
Joseph Hamilton
William C. Jennings
Mrs. William Manger
Richard J. Murphy
Nicholas A. Pace, M.D.
The Reverend Daniel O'Hare
Mrs. R. Randolph Richardson
Mrs. Jason Robards
George K. Russell, Ph.D.
Lt. Gen. Robert G. Yerks, USA (Ret)

OFFICERS
M. G. H. Gilliam, Esq.
Chairman
Nicholas A. Pace, M.D.
Vice Chairman
George K. Russell, Ph.D.
Secretary
William C. Jennings
Treasurer

STAFF
Lee I. Dogoloff
Executive Director
Ellen E. Newman
Director of Development

SCIENTIFIC ADVISORY BOARD
Robert G. Heath, M.D.
(Chairman)
Professor and Chief of
 Psychiatry and Neurology
Tulane University Medical School

Robert L. DuPont, M.D.
(President)
Former Director of National Institute
 on Drug Abuse

Henry Brill, M.D.
Clinical Professor of Psychiatry
New York State
University at Stony Brook

Jose Carranza, M.D.
Clinical Associate Professor
Baylor College of Medicine

Sidney Cohen, M.D., Ph.D.
Clinical Professor of Psychiatry
Neuropsychiatric Institute
UCLA

Professor Sir William D.M. Paton
Professor and Chairman
Institute of Pharmacology
Oxford University

Robert C. Petersen, Ph.D.
Research Psychologist

Carol G. Smith, Ph.D.
Associate Professor of
 Pharmacology
Uniformed Services University
 of the Health Sciences

Harold Voth, M.D.
Chief of Staff
Veterans Administration Medical Center
Topeka, Kansas

For further information, contact:
ACDE
5820 Hubbard Drive
Rockville, Maryland 20852